{ focus on
plot +
themes of }   Me
rev.

not rev. personality? 1990

everyone   { have st read only chap
reads 1st ← { in Rowbotham (Russia,
5 chaps however China, Africa) that
Structure course   applies to their own
                        proj.

1. Bondage – tyranny
   sit. of women in
   France before Rev.
   and in 1789 (cahiers
   de doléances) → texts

   2. Wilderness – murmurings
      (still slave mentality)

#Rowbotham – austerity + vs "freedom"
"ph love in laws   of old bondage
early Rev. necessary transition tyranny + licence
           violence / need for education period
women's ← 3. revolutionary purge (Terror) of Girondins
history in this Covenant. Does this covenant
           apply to women? "liberté, égalité,
                    fraternité"
   Déclaration des droits de la femme …
#Women included in covenant,
but as wives.
   4. Promised Land –   and those
      visions of future   not
                        "committed"
      realized?   to rev.

      men's vs women's
           vision
      (public vs private)

   $109 repub of virtue

112 Fr Rev

Exodus and Revolution

1st day "Exodus"
reggae music

theoretical basis
for notion of
revolution

EXODUS AND REVOLUTION

Michael Walzer

Basic Books, Inc., Publishers

NEW YORK

Library of Congress Cataloging in Publication Data

Walzer, Michael.
    Exodus and revolution.

    Includes bibliographical references and index.
    1. Exodus, The—Typology.   2. Revolution (Theology)
I. Title.
BS680.E9W35   1984   222'.12064   84–45306
ISBN   0–465–02164–6 (cloth)
ISBN   0–465–02163–8 (paper)

For Martin Peretz

CONTENTS

PREFACE

THIS IS A BOOK about an idea of great presence and power in Western political thought, the idea of a deliverance from suffering and oppression: this-worldly redemption, liberation, revolution. I have sought to describe the origins of that idea in the story of Israel's deliverance from Egypt and then to give a reading of Exodus, Numbers, and Deuteronomy designed to explain their importance for generation after generation of religious and political radicals. The escape from bondage, the wilderness journey, the Sinai covenant, the promised land: all these loom large in the literature of revolution. Indeed, revolution has often been imagined as an enactment of the Exodus and the Exodus has often been imagined as a program for revolution. I want to pursue these imaginings, for they illuminate (although they don't tell the whole truth about) both the ancient books and the characteristically modern forms of political action. So I move back and forth between the biblical narrative (and the most authoritative commentaries), on the one hand, and the tracts and treatises, the slogans and songs, of radical politics, on the other. I move back and forth, that is, between a field of study where I am an amateur and a novice and a field of study where I have some professional experience. I hope that the enthusiasm of the amateur and the caution of the professional will somehow balance one another. But if I err, let it be on the side of enthusiasm, for we still have much to learn, I think, from a close study of the Exodus.

It is not my purpose to provide a history of the idea of deliverance but a study of its meaning, and there is no better way to get at that meaning than to imitate the many advocates and activists of deliverance who have gathered their followers around them and read the biblical story. Read and expounded and interpreted the story: for every reading is also a construction, a reinvention of the past for the sake of the present. But why is this story so endlessly reinvented? That is what I have tried to explain.

Most of the reinventions have been the work of religious men and women who found in the text not only a record of God's actions in the world but also a guide for His people—which is to say, themselves. Perhaps they were wrong, but that is not for me to argue. Within the sacred history of the Exodus, they discovered a vivid and realistic secular history that helped them to understand their own political activity. I shall repeat that discovery. I don't mean to disparage the sacred, only to explore the secular: my subject is not what God has done but what men and women have done, first with the biblical text itself and then in the world, with the text in their hands.

I have worked almost entirely in English. I can make my way through the Hebrew of the biblical books but not of the Midrash or the medieval Jewish commentaries. Fortunately, much of this latter material now exists in translation, including the entire *Midrash Rabbah*, the *Mekilta De-Rabbi Ishmael* (a commentary on Exod. 12–23), Rashi's notes on the biblical text, and the commentaries of Nachmanides. In my use of untranslated material, I have relied on Louis Ginzberg's *Legends of the Jews* and Nehama Leibowitz's excellent *Studies in Exodus, Studies in Numbers,* and *Studies in Deuteronomy.* I am sure that I have missed a great deal—not only in ancient and medieval books but also in the work of contemporary Israeli scholars. But at some point in any case I would have had to put aside other people's interpretations and address the text and its political uses directly. In fact, I began to do that a long time ago, for my bar mitzvah portion was *Ki Tissa* (Exod. 30:-11–34:35), which includes the story of the golden calf, and I worried then, as many more learned readers had worried before me, about Moses' command to kill the idol worshippers. At that time I took Hobbes's view (as reported in Aubrey's *Lives*) and argued with my teacher "against the cruelty of Moses for putting so many thousands to the sword." It is an argument I want to continue, though now with a larger purpose.

In quoting the biblical text I have used the King James translation, the most familiar and still the most eloquent version, and (together with the Geneva Bible) the version read by the English and American revolutionaries to whose works I shall often refer. Occasionally, I have provided an alternative translation or a brief explanation of a particularly important word or phrase, but mostly I have let the text stand. I cannot pretend to be a scholar of ancient languages. But the failure to grasp the precise meaning of this or that word has never obscured, nor will it do so now, the liberating vision of the Exodus story.

I first read the biblical text in 1948 with Rabbi Hayim Goren Perelmuter, a teacher of exemplary understanding and contagious enthusiasm; I still recall our discussions, in which this book had a kind of beginning. Its nearer origin is in three lectures given in 1983 at Princeton University's Gauss Seminar, and I am grateful to Joseph Frank, who presided over the seminar, for his encouragement and support. I gave the lectures again at the City University of New York (under the sponsorship of the Center for Jewish Studies) and at Indiana University (as the Patten Lectures), and I read a version of chapter 2 at the University of Chicago and at Hebrew University in

Jerusalem. On all these occasions, there were lively and helpful arguments; I have tried to incorporate or respond to some of these, especially the arguments of Marshall Berman, Theodore Draper, Jerrold Siegel, and Bernard Yack.

Aaron Wildavsky's *The Nursing Father: Moses as a Political Leader* (Alabama, 1984) appeared too late for me to cite it here, but I did read and learn from an early draft. I have drawn freely on two articles of my own dealing with the central themes of this book, one in the *Harvard Theological Review,* one in the Harvard Hillel journal *Mosaic,* both published in 1968.

Moshe Greenberg, David Hartman, Irving Howe, Seth Schein, Judith Walzer, Sally Walzer, and Leon Wieseltier read the entire manuscript at different stages and provided detailed criticism and numerous suggestions, some of which I have been wise enough to accept. I sat writing the book at the Institute for Advanced Study whose faculty and members were a resident audience, a crucial source of ideas, references, and cautions. Long walks and conversations with Allan Silver, who was at the Institute in 1982–83, helped to give the book its present shape. Lynda Emery typed and retyped (processed and reprocessed) the manuscript and is responsible for whatever consistency in grammar and spelling I have achieved: the errors that remain are those that I have insisted upon.

Reading, arguing, talking about the Exodus, in this country and in Israel, over the last few years, I have found to my delight that the story, even in these latter times, is still a part of our common culture. Though everyone has his own version, it is a story that we all share.

Princeton, New Jersey
August 1984

INTRODUCTION

Exodus History

I

IN the early months of 1960, I visited a number of southern cities in order to write about the black student sit-ins that marked, though I didn't know it then, the beginning of sixties radicalism. And in Montgomery, Alabama, in a small Baptist church, I listened to the most extraordinary sermon that I have ever heard—on the Book of Exodus and the political struggle of southern blacks. There on his pulpit, the preacher, whose name I have long forgotten, acted out the "going out" from Egypt and expounded its contemporary analogues: he cringed under the lash, challenged the pharaoh, hesitated fearfully at the sea, accepted the covenant and the law at the foot of the mountain.[1] The sermon struck me with especial force because I was, in 1960, a graduate student writing a dissertation on the Puritan Revolution, and I had read many sermons in which the Book of Exodus figured as a central text or a reiterated reference. Indeed, in a long speech opening the first session of the first elected parliament of his protectorship, Oliver Cromwell described the Exodus as "the only parallel of God's dealing with us that I know in the world. . . ." The parallel was not yet complete: "We are thus far, through the mercy of God, . . ." said Cromwell, and warned against the return to "bondage under the regal power" that in fact followed close upon his own death four years later.[2] The Montgomery preacher presumably hoped for a more sustained parallel, and I hoped with him and decided then to write about the Exodus and its political significance.

Since then, not surprisingly, I have found the Exodus almost everywhere, often in unexpected places. It is central to the communist theology or antitheology of Ernst Bloch, the source and original of his "principle of hope" ("We are thus far," said Cromwell, "a door of hope is open. . . .").[3] It is the subject of a book by Lincoln Steffens, called *Moses in Red*, published in 1926: a detailed account of Israel's political struggles in the wilderness and a defense of Leninist politics.[4] It plays a large part in the "liberation theology" worked out by Catholic priests in Latin America. In the 1970s, the most serious and sustained work on the Exodus was probably being done in countries like Argentina, Peru, and Colombia. "If we take the Exodus as our theme," wrote the Argentine theologian Severino Croatto, "we do so because in it Latin American theology finds a focal point . . . and an inexhaustible light."[5] Wherever people know the Bible, and experience oppression, the Exodus has sustained their spirits and (sometimes) inspired their resistance. Certainly, the Montgomery preacher was working in a long tradition, which reaches back to the days of slavery and includes not only hope but also celebration:

> Shout the glad tidings o'er
> Egypt's dark sea,

4

> Jehovah has triumphed, his people
> are free![6]

But in 1960, they weren't free, and the preacher had to recognize that the Exodus did not happen once and for all, that liberation is no guarantee of liberty—an idea that appears also in the earliest Jewish interpretations of the Exodus story, in Deuteronomy and the Prophets. In fact, the return to Egypt is part of the story, though it exists in the text only as a possibility: that's why the story can be retold so often.

So common is the Exodus reference in the political history of the West (or, at least, of protest and radical aspiration in the West) that I began to notice when it was missing—as in the years of the French Revolution, whose leading actors were resolutely hostile to Jewish as they were to Christian conceptions of history. Hostile, but not ignorant: when a member of the Committee of Public Safety announced that the terror would have to be endured for "thirty to fifty years," he was, I suspect, making a disguised reference to the forty years of Israelite wandering in the wilderness (and also to the conventional understanding of the reasons for that long detour on what might have been a short journey).[7] In any case, the text is a common reference point before and after 1789. It figures prominently in medieval debates over the legitimacy of crusading warfare. It is important to the political argument of the radical monk Savonarola, who preached twenty-two sermons on the Book of Exodus in the months just before his fall and execution. It is cited in the pamphlets of the German peasants' revolt. John Calvin and John Knox justified their most extreme political positions by quoting from Exodus. The text underpins the radical contractualism of the Huguenot *Vindiciae Contra*

Tyrannos and then of the Scottish Presbyterians.[8] It is crucial, as I have already suggested, to the self-understanding of the English Puritans during the 1640s, and of the Americans, too, on their "errand into the wilderness." It is an important source of both argument and symbolism during the American Revolution and the establishment on these shores of "God's new Israel." In 1776, Benjamin Franklin proposed that the Great Seal of the United States should show Moses with his rod lifted and the Egyptian army drowning in the sea; while Jefferson urged a more pacific design: the column of Israelites marching through the wilderness led by God's pillars of cloud and fire.[9] The Exodus story is important in the writings of that early socialist, Moses Hess, and it figures, though only occasionally and marginally, in the political writings of Karl Marx. And, of course, the Exodus has always stood at the very center of Jewish religious thought and has played a part in each of the reiterated attempts at a Jewish politics, from the Maccabean revolt to the Zionist movement. Zionism has sometimes been conceived in messianic terms, which both derive from and stand in tension with Exodus thinking; but it is also a call for a literal exodus —an escape from oppression and a journey to the promised land—and the biblical narrative has provided much of its imagery. Other nationalisms, too, have found hope in a promise that seems to include, whatever else it includes, the idea of political independence. The Book of Exodus came alive in the hands of Boer nationalists fighting the British, and it is alive in the hands of black nationalists in South Africa today.[10]

When I began to work on this book, long after my visit to Montgomery, my intention was to give an account of the political history of the Exodus story, to describe the ways in which the story was used, the purposes it served, over the years. But I have decided now to attempt something bolder than that and to make larger claims than would be possible within a purely historical account. I want to retell the story as it figures in political history, to read the text in the light of its interpretations, to discover its meaning in what it has meant. I want to argue that the uses of the text have not been violations, not inventions or mere inventions, and that the Exodus as we know it in the text is plausibly understood in political terms, as a liberation and a revolution—even though it is also, in the text, an act of God. "Have we paid sufficient attention," Croatto asks, "to the fact that the first, exemplary liberation event, which 'reveals' the God of salvation, was political and social?"[11] I shall pay attention, and expound the Exodus as a paradigm of revolutionary politics. But the word "paradigm" is to be taken loosely here: the Exodus isn't a theory of revolution, and it would make little sense to try to construct a theory out of the biblical account. The Exodus is a story, a big story, one that became part of the cultural consciousness of the West—so that a range of political events (different events, but a particular range) have been located and understood within the narrative frame that it provides. This story made it possible to tell other stories.

In returning to the original text, I make no claims about the substantive intentions of its authors and editors, and I commit myself to no specific view of the actual history. What really happened? We don't know. We have only this story, written down centuries after the events it describes. But the story is more important than the events, and the story has grown more and more important as it has been repeated and reflected upon, cited in arguments, elaborated in folklore. Perhaps that was the intention of the authors: certainly, they urge the repetition often

7

enough. The Exodus belongs to a genre of religious and legal texts designed for public reading and rereading and for analogical application. The authors of such texts, whoever they are, cannot expect to exercise close control over their meanings. Unless, of course, the author is God: but God has obviously chosen not to exercise close control, and we must assume, along with one of the central strands of Jewish interpretation, that He intends all the meanings that He has made us capable of discovering.[12] I shall consider only one of those meanings. But that one —Exodus as revolution—has had a consistent place in the interpretive literature over many centuries. It also has a firm foundation in the actual words of Exodus and Numbers.

Those words I shall read straightforwardly, as they occur. There are occasional confusions and obscurities in the text that has come down to us, but by and large the literary artfulness of the final authors and editors has produced a remarkably coherent narrative. The effort of modern critics to disentangle authorial traditions, to identify earlier and later fragments within the narrative, has not in my view produced a better understanding of the Exodus story, certainly not of the story as it has been read and reread, cited and elaborated. "At no point," as Northrop Frye has written, "does [this effort] throw any real light on how or why a poet might read the bible"—and it is no more help to a political theorist.[13] Of course, in the tradition of commentary and citation to which I shall be referring, the text was also broken into fragments; every sentence, every phrase, was conceived to be God's word, capable of sustaining independent interpretation. But these fragments were at the same time understood as parts of a whole, and if we fail to respect the whole, we will fail, very often, to grasp the deepest meaning of the interpretations.

Perhaps, however, we should separate early and late interpretations and assign special value to the oldest readings of the story by the Deuteronomic writers and the Prophets. Some principle of nearness seems to require recognition here, though it is immediately necessary to add that even the earliest of the Prophets did not share the circumstances or the sensibilities of the people who first told the Exodus story, even of the people who first wrote it down; and they could only imagine the experiences that the text describes. And it would be a mistake to devalue those later readers—like Savonarola or Cromwell—who came to the text with their private occasions, so to speak, in their hands. For they could have come as well to many other texts but chose this one, finding in its words some lively echo of their own political necessities, their own realism, their own vision of the future. We can only ask whether their readings make the words more intelligible, more luminous for us.

The Exodus is an account of deliverance or liberation expressed in religious terms, but it is also a secular, that is, a this-worldly and historical account. Most important, it is a realistic account, in which miracles play a part but which is not itself miraculous. Were the story wholly miraculous, there would be no point to the interpretation I shall defend. Or, I would need to "see through" the miracles to some putative human reality behind them— imitating the contemporary theologian who writes that the biblical emphasis on divine intervention "is peculiar to religious *language;* it does not mean that this is the way [the Exodus] occurred historically." What the text tells us is simply that "a liberation process having all the contours

myth

of a political event can very well be interpreted—indeed should be interpreted for a Christian conscience—as the will of God."[14] This does not seem to me the best strategy for reading the story: far better to see where divine intervention is decisive and where it is not. The Israelites are not, after all, magically transported to the promised land; they are not carried on the "eagle's wings" of Exodus 19; they must march to get there, and the march is full of difficulties, crises, struggles, all realistically presented, as if to invite human as well as divine resolution. In an early rabbinic commentary on Exodus, the famous sage Judah Ha-Nasi is quoted as saying: "Through the strength of God Israel went out of Egypt, as it is said: 'By strength of hand, the Lord brought us out of Egypt.'" But, the commentary continues, there is "another interpretation": "With an alertness of their own Israel went out of Egypt, as it is said: 'And thus shall ye eat [the paschal lamb], with your loins girded, your shoes on your feet, and your staff in your hand.'"[15] I sympathize with the second interpretation, though in this case it strains the text; in any case, the two are not contradictory. Many men and women, believing in God's mighty hand, have nevertheless girded their loins, challenged the pharaohs of their own time, marched into the wilderness—and understood what they were doing by reading Exodus. Now I shall try to understand the story they read and retold to one another.

II

THE STORY (I mean now the whole story, not just that part of it contained in the Book of Exodus) is a classic narrative, with a beginning, a middle, and an end: problem, struggle, resolution—Egypt, the wilderness, the promised land. My chapters reflect this simple structure, though I divide the story of the wilderness years, separating out two things that are in fact closely connected: the murmurings and the covenant. But before I get to the beginning and try to understand Egyptian oppression, I need to say something about the character and strength of the narrative line. For the movement from beginning to end is the key to the historical importance of the Exodus story. The strength of the narrative is given by the end, though it is also crucial that the end be present at the beginning, as an aspiration, a hope, a promise. What is promised is radically different from what is: the end is nothing like the beginning. This is an obvious but critical point. The Exodus bears no resemblance to those ancient tales of voyages and journeys that, whatever the adventures they include, begin and end at home. It's not like the journey of the eleventh-century Egyptian priest Wen-Amon to Byblos in Phoenicia and then, after many difficulties, back (though the narrative breaks off while he is on his way) to his temple at Karnak.[16] Nor can it be described as an odyssey, a long wandering such as Homer recounted, at the end of which wait wife and child (and ancient servant and faithful dog). According to the biblical story, only Joseph's bones return to Canaan; for the living Israelites the promised land is a new home, and no one is waiting there to greet them. In the literature of the ancient world only the *Aeneid* resembles the Exodus in its narrative structure, describing a divinely guided and world-historical journey to something like a promised land.[17] That is why the *Aeneid* was the only rival of the Exodus in the arguments over the American Great Seal. But Rome, though it represents for Virgil a "new order of the ages," is not, after all, significantly different from

Troy; it is only more powerful; while Canaan is the very opposite of Egypt.

The Israelites do not, as is sometimes said, go wandering in the wilderness; the Exodus is a journey forward—not only in time and space. It is a march toward a goal, a moral progress, a transformation. The men and women who reach Canaan are, literally and figuratively, not the same men and women who left Egypt. The subject of the march is the "people of Israel," a phrase first used in the first chapter of the Book of Exodus. Genesis is a collection of stories about individual men and women; they are mostly members of one family, a family, moreover, with a singular destiny; but we are focused on individuals. Exodus, by contrast, is the story of a people, hence not a story simply but a history.[18] Though Moses plays a critical role in that history (less so in its later repetitions), the people are central. And Moses' importance is not personal but political—as leader of the people or mediator between the people and God—for this is a *political* history: it is about slavery and freedom, law and rebellion. Like the march that it describes, the history, too, has a goal. It is, as William Irwin has written, "history told from a determined point of view and with a set purpose."[19] That purpose is to teach the importance of the march and the discipline necessary to its success.

A political history with a strong linearity, a strong forward movement, the Exodus gives permanent shape to Jewish conceptions of time; and it serves as a model, ultimately, for non-Jewish conceptions too. We can think of it as the crucial alternative to all mythic notions of eternal recurrence—and hence to those cyclical understandings of political change from which our word "revolution" derives. The idea of eternal recurrence connects the social to the natural world and gives to political life the simple

12

closure of a circle: birth, maturity, death, and rebirth. The same story is enacted again and again; men and women and the timely deeds of men and women alike lose their singularity; one represents another in a system of correspondences that extends upward, hierarchically, into the mythic realm of nature and of nature's gods. Biblical narrative generally, Exodus more particularly, breaks in the most decisive way with this kind of cosmological storytelling.[20] In Exodus history events occur only once, and they take on their significance from a system of backward- and forward-looking interconnections, not from the hierarchical correspondences of myth.

linear time

Consider for a moment the "murmurings," which I will take up in detail in chapter 2. According to one count (in Num. 14:22), there were ten of these occasions on which the people complained, perhaps rebelled, against Moses, though not all of them begin with the standard phrase (first used in Exod. 15:24), "And the people murmured against Moses. . . ." I suppose the number ten is meant to match the plagues and the commandments. The pattern of the murmurings is repetitious and to some extent stereotyped, and yet each of the incidents is different from all the others, and the set can plausibly be read as a progressive series, or a doubled series, culminating in the story of the golden calf and again in the great rebellion of Numbers 14. "It is probable," writes Martin Buber, "that certain of these narratives are only 'doublets' and can be attributed to varying traditions of the same event."[21] Perhaps so, but the repeated narratives also advance the story. In Exodus 15, for example, the people come to Marah, three days' march from the Red Sea, and find the water there bitter: "And the people murmured against Moses, saying, What shall we drink?" Some weeks later, at Rephidim, there was no water at all:

"Wherefore the people chided Moses, and said, Give us water that we may drink" (Exod. 17:2). "Chided" is *va-yarev*, better translated as "opposed" or "contended with": the text suggests an escalation of fear and anger that closely parallels the greater danger. The theme of popular fearfulness—central to Exodus history—isn't merely reiterated; it is developed and expanded.

Similarly, one can say that Egypt or at least Egyptian-like oppression recurs again and again in the larger history of Israel. But the recurrence is always explained in moral and political, never in cosmological, terms. It is a result of backsliding along a temporal line. When the Israelites find themselves oppressed in their own land, it is because, as the prophet Jeremiah tells them, "their transgressions are many and their backslidings have increased" (5:6). Oppression isn't determined or inevitable, like fall's decline and winter's death; it isn't the repeated manifestation of a characterological flaw; it follows from particular choices by particular people—a failure of moral alertness, a willful refusal to "remember" the house of bondage and the day of deliverance, a violation of divine commandments. The appeal of Exodus history to generations of radicals lies in its linearity, in the idea of a promised end, in the purposiveness of the Israelite march. The movement across space is readily reconstructed as a movement from one political regime to another. (I should note that the same reconstruction also works for personal change: thus John Bunyan's *Pilgrim's Progress*, the tale of a journey from the worldly city, through the wilderness of the world, to a place called Jerusalem—and also a tale of self-transformation.) Change of position is a common metaphor for change of regime; much of the political language of the left has its origin in that metaphor—not only battle cries like *"Marchons!"* or "Forward!" or poems like William Morris's "March of the Workers,"[22]

> Forth they come from grief and torment,
> on they wend toward health and mirth,

but also articles and essays about progress, progressive parties, advanced ideas, vanguard politics, revolution (in its current sense), movement itself, as in "the labor movement," a phrase that has nothing to do, any more than Morris's poem does, with geographic mobility but rather describes the organization of the workers for radical politics.

Exodus is a literal movement, an advance through space and time, the original form of (or formula for) progressive history. This, I confess immediately, is a revisionist view that I can only assert here and not defend. Scholars most often trace the origins of strong linearity to later Jewish and Christian eschatologies, to the apocalyptic doctrines of Daniel and Revelation.[23] These texts suggest both a cosmic history, which moves from creation to redemption, and a political history, which moves from worldly tyranny (identified now with that second Egypt, the Babylonia of the Exile) to messianic kingdom. The two movements, and the enthusiasm they engender in those who glimpse the End, are readily contrasted with the more melancholy views of Stoic philosophers like Chrysippus or political historians like Polybius, for whom the world turns in fixed circles, and no change can ever represent a genuine advance.[24] The seeds of the eighteenth- and nineteenth-century idea of progress are similarly found in the revival of millenarian thought in the late medieval and early modern periods (as against the revival of cyclical thought in the Renaissance). The radical politics of our own time, which seizes on the idea of progress and the hope of redemption, is identified as a secular millenarianism, a political messianism, and traced back to Joachim of Fiore and to the chiliastic sects of the Reformation.[25] Indeed, it is only in the early modern period that the word "revolution" begins to take on the meaning that it has for contemporary militants: a one-way and once-and-for-all transformation of the political world. But this account misses an earlier stage of intellectual development and, what may be more important, an alternative conception of political change.

Messianism comes late in Jewish history, and it comes, I think, by way of Exodus thinking. "We judge the promise of final Redemption," wrote the ninth-century philosopher Saadya Gaon, "from the first promise at the time when we were living as exiles in Egypt."[26] The end of days does not figure in Jewish thought until sometime after the Babylonian exile, but speculation about the end consistently looks back, as Saadya suggests, to the earlier "exile" in Egypt. The final redemption is the original redemption writ large. It is often preceded, in Jewish versions, by a new Exodus, a second Moses, the reappearance of manna, and so on.[27] Now, however, the divine promise is reinterpreted to describe a "new heaven and a new earth" rather than the familiar land of Canaan and to offer delights even greater, if there are delights greater, than milk and honey. In Christianity, too, an effort is made to fit the messianic story to the Exodus pattern. The Christ-child is saved from a slaughter of infants, so that Jesus can be called a latter-day Moses, and Herod a latter-day Pharaoh. And the crucial numbers reappear: twelve disciples to match the twelve tribes, forty days in the wilderness to match the forty years. But the Exodus also has its own integrity. Moses, after all, is not a messiah; he is a political leader who succeeds in bringing the Israelites out of Egypt but is unable to bring them into the promised land. Nor is the promised land the same thing as the messianic kingdom (not at least as the messianic kingdom is commonly understood): the difference between these two is one of the chief themes of chapter 4. Exodus is a model for messianic and millenarian thought, and it is also a standing alternative to it—a secular and historical account of "redemption," an account that does not require the miraculous transformation of the material world but sets God's people marching through the world toward a better place within it. It isn't a coincidence, then, that Oliver Cromwell, in the same speech in which he invoked the Exodus as the only parallel in world history to God's dealings with the English, also broke decisively with the visionary politics of the Fifth Monarchy (the reign of King Jesus). Cromwell understood that the march through the wilderness required nothing more than a leader like himself.

The march does not lie beyond history; the leader is only a man—and a limited man at that, who needs Aaron to speak (and Miriam to sing) on his behalf. Later on, he needs the "rulers of thousands, and rulers of hundreds, rulers of fifties, and rulers of tens" whose appointment Jethro recommends: "for this thing is too heavy for thee; thou art not able to perform it thyself alone" (Exod. 18:18, 21). No one has ever spoken in similar terms about the messiah who, whatever he does, does it without political assistance. The Exodus is an event cut to a human scale, and so it echoes not only in the literature of the millennium but also in historical and political literature. If we listen closely to the echoes, we can "hear" the Exodus as a story of radical hope and this-worldly endeavor.

ONE

The House of Bondage:

Slaves in Egypt

I

THE strength of Exodus history lies in its end, the divine promise. It is also true, of course, that the significance and value of the end is given by the beginning. Canaan is a promised land because Egypt is a house of bondage. Beginning and end stand in a necessary relation. The Exodus is not a lucky escape from misfortune. Rather, the misfortune has a moral character, and the escape has a world-historical meaning. Egypt is not just left behind; it is rejected; it is judged and condemned. The crucial terms of that judgment are *oppression* and *corruption*, and I shall examine each of these in turn. But I must stress first that the judgment is conceivable only because of the promise; its moral force requires the idea, at least, of a life that is neither oppressive nor corrupt. God's promise generates a sense of possibility (it would be rash, given the fearfulness of the Israelite slaves, to say that it generates a sense of confidence): the world is not all Egypt. Without that sense of possibility, oppression would be experienced as an inescapable condition, a matter of personal or collective bad luck, a stroke of fate. There are indeed religious standpoints from which one can judge the world as a whole and find it oppressive and corrupt—Satan's world. But Pharaoh is not Satan, and the biblical judgment is not of that sort. Its moral quality depends upon the existence of alternative possibilities here and now. Anger and hope, not resignation, are the appropriate responses to the Egyptian house of bondage.

The point can be made more forcefully by way of a comparison. Euripides' *Women of Troy* provides a useful contrast with the Exodus story, for it describes a "going out" that leads to slavery rather than to freedom. Thus, Hecabe, at the end of the play:

> Come, trembling aged feet,
> You must not fail me now.
> There your way lies: forward into slavery![1]

The women have been abandoned by the gods of their city. For them there is no promise. "I have not even the common human blessing of hope," says Andromache; "I cannot delude myself with the pleasant dream of . . . happiness in the future."[2] Without illusion, the women steadfastly confront (and bewail) their destiny. Slavery is the natural consequence of defeat; the Greeks exult, the women weep: everyone behaves as expected.

Euripides makes no moral judgment; at least, he makes no judgment of the slavery into which the woman are led. The feeling that he means to evoke is pity, not anger or indignation. We are, perhaps, invited to be angry at particular acts of cruelty—the murders of Hecabe's daughter and of Andromache's (and Hector's) son. But we are meant above all to pity the women, particularly the noble women, for whom slavery is an agony of the soul. In aristocratic eyes, the loss of freedom is "the height of disgrace," as a modern historian writes, and also, mixing his metaphors, "a sudden fall into the void."[3] Euripides wants to remind his contemporaries, who have just enslaved the women of Melos, of how sudden such falls can be. Bondage is certainly oppressive in his portrayal, but it is not unjust. It is oppressive like a hot and humid summer day—infinitely worse, of course, but like that nonetheless. Slavery, to quote the dictionary now, "lies heavy on, weighs down, crushes the feelings, mind, spirits. . . ."[4] This is the argument of the play; what Euripides has written is the long lament of the Trojan women.

The language of Exodus is sometimes similar in tone. Slavery is described in the first chapters of the book as an "affliction," a "burden," a "sorrow." Clearly, the Israelites found slavery oppressive, just as the Greeks did. But the Greeks also found war and disease, sieges and fevers oppressive; they consistently used the word *piezein,* derived (like the Hebrew *lachatz*) from a root meaning "to press down," in a nonmoral sense. In the literature of fifth- and fourth-century Athens (B.C.E.), so far as I can tell, the word is standardly used in the passive voice and always with an impersonal subject: "oppressed by war," "oppressed by fever."[5] By contrast, biblical usage is active and personal. It is crucial to the Exodus story and explicit in the text that Pharaoh and his taskmasters oppressed the children of Israel. "Behold," God says to Moses, "I have seen the oppression wherewith the Egyptians oppress them" (Exod. 3:9). The dictionary puts the two definitions, impersonal and personal, passive and active, side by side, but it is this second meaning that has been so important in the political history of the West: "to keep under by tyrannical exercise of power, to burden . . . with cruel or unjust impositions or restraints."[6]

Perhaps I should be more careful. Pharaoh is never explicitly called a tyrant in the Book of Exodus, though he is known ever after in Jewish literature as the first of the tyrants. The warnings about the dangers of kingship in Deuteronomy 17 and First Samuel 8 obviously look back to Pharaoh's Egypt. Nor is the oppression of the Israelites actually called unjust (it is called cruel). One of the Hebrew words sometimes translated as oppression ('ani, also, and better, translated as "affliction") more nearly expresses misery and pain than wrongful injury. And yet the wrongfulness of Israel's bondage is surely the argument of the text. So the text has been read, at any rate, from the earliest times. Thus, it is commonly said that when Moses killed the Egyptian taskmaster, he acted rightly, punishing a wrongdoer. Some of the rabbis worried that the punishment was excessive, since the taskmaster had not killed, but only beaten, the Israelite slave; but even they agreed that Moses' anger was righteous.[7] It is a good thing to stand against oppression. Much of the moral code of the Torah is explained and defended in opposition to Egyptian cruelty. The Israelites are commanded to act justly, which is to say, not as the Egyptians acted; and the motive of their action is to be the memory of the injustice their ancestors suffered in Egypt and which they suffer again, through the remembering, in the Egypt of their minds.

The new regime is defined by contrast with the old. Not only *this* new regime, the commonwealth founded by Moses: in an important sense, the language of revolutionary politics generally (and of religious messianism, too) is first developed and deployed here. Oppression takes on the moral significance it has had in the Judeo-Christian world ever since. And the possibility of deliverance and redemption is decisively broached. The word "redemption" derives, in Hebrew as in English, from a legal term meaning "to buy back"—in this case, the freedom of a slave. The Hebrew noun translated as "deliverance" comes from the verb "to go out." But it is only if one goes out from Egypt (not, say, from Troy) that one is delivered. In England in the 1640s, "deliverance" played roughly the same role as "liberation" plays today: the two words are closely related, and like "redemption" they take their larger meanings from the experience of slavery. It may be the case that other experiences of slavery have generated similar meanings. When the Spartan helots, for example, whose condition in some ways resembled that of Israel in Egypt, rebelled against their masters, we can be certain that they aimed to set themselves free.[8] But we don't know what they made of their freedom once they had won it, with Theban help, in 371 B.C.E. Did they "remember" their bondage when they celebrated their deliverance? Did they shape a new politics in the light of that memory? Probably they did not, for slavery was a degraded and shameful condition in ancient Greece, and former slaves tried most often to escape their past, to forget rather than to remember. In any case, we have no account of the helot idea of deliverance; nor did that idea, whatever it was, have any further influence; whereas it is possible to trace a continuous history from the Exodus to the radical politics of our own time.

II

I WON'T try to do that, however; I want to focus instead on what happened in Egypt. What was the nature of the oppression? Certainly, it wasn't slavery itself, at least, not chattel slavery. The Israelites were not bought and sold in Egypt; nor is slavery in this sense barred (though it is extensively regulated) in the legal code that comes out of the Exodus experience. We might better say that the Israelites were guests in Egypt, later on, guest workers, later on still, state slaves, subjected to a kind of *corvée*. Many Egyptians were similarly subject; that's why Egypt was called a "house of bondage" (literally: house of slaves). What features of the house of bondage do we highlight when we describe it as tyrannical? What specifically were its unjust impositions? Why did Egyptian bondage become the original and archetypal form of oppression?

The easiest modern reading of the first chapter of the Book of Exodus is social and economic in character; we are accustomed to think of oppression in those terms. Lincoln Steffens provides a nice example when he calls Moses a "loyal labor leader."[9] A contemporary Latin American priest describes the suffering of the Israelites under four headings: repression, alienated work, humiliation, and enforced birth control.[10] That last phrase might refer to a midrashic story according to which the Egyptians worked their male slaves so hard and long that they could not return to their wives at night but fell asleep, exhausted, in their workplaces.[11] Or it might refer—though the euphemism would be a bit odd for a theologian of liberation —to Pharaoh's order to the midwives to kill the newborn sons of the Israelites. This is infanticide, not birth control; its purpose was to destroy the entire people of Israel by destroying the male line, leaving a population of women and girls to be dispersed as slaves among Egyptian households. I won't say much more about this aspect of Pharaoh's policy. Among Jews it has come to be seen as the first of a series of attempts on Jewish peoplehood that culminates in the Nazi death camps. Indeed, the Pharaoh of the oppression does sound oddly like a modern anti-Semite, worrying (in Exod. 1:10) about the growing power of the Israelites, who had prospered in Egypt, and their possible disloyalty: "lest they join also unto our enemies. . . . " But it isn't the killing of the sons that figures in the earliest discussions of the Exodus story in Deuteronomy and the Prophets. Nor is the killing central to non-Jewish understandings of Egyptian bondage—not, at least, until Catholic priests began to take an interest in liberation. [Nor does this part of the story make the persistent longing of the Israelites to return to Egypt easy to understand.] One can, indeed, pine for one's oppressor, but not for the murderer of one's children.

The central tradition focuses on the *corvée,* not on the attempted genocide. "And they made their lives bitter with hard bondage, in mortar, and in brick, and in all manner of service in the field; all their service, wherein they made them serve, was with rigor" (Exod. 1:14). The Hebrew word for "with rigor" is *be-farech,* and it occurs only one other time in the Torah, in Leviticus 25, where the laws for the treatment of Israelite slaves are laid down: "Thou shalt not rule over [them] with rigor," that is, as the Egyptians did. Many years later Maimonides effectively extended this protection to all slaves, and at the same time he offered a definition of *be-farech.* Rigorous service, he suggested, is service without the limits of time or purpose.[12] Bondage involves work without end; hence it is work that both exhausts and degrades the slave. Writing in the sixteenth century, the author of the *Vindiciae* takes a similar view: the tyrant, he says, "erects idle and needless trophies to continually employ his tributaries, that they might want leisure to think on other things, as Pharaoh did the Jews. . . . "[13] Because of what Pharaoh did, perhaps, biblical legislation sets a limit on the term of enslavement—though a limit that applies only to Israelite slaves: "If thou buy an Hebrew servant, six years he shall serve: and in the seventh he shall go out free for nothing" (Exod. 21:2). We don't know if the limit was ever enforced, but it was not forgotten. The prophet Jeremiah blames the fall of Judea and the Babylonian exile on the failure of the people to "proclaim liberty" to enslaved brothers and neighbors after six years, as they had covenanted to do, he says, when God brought them up out of Egypt (34:8–23). It may be that the freedom of the seventh day—an easier matter—was more widely accepted than the freedom of the seventh year. In Deuteronomy, the reason given for the establishment of the Sabbath is "that thy manservant and thy maidservant may rest as well as thou . . . remember that thou wast a servant in the land of Egypt" (Deut. 5:14; see also Exod. 23:12). This commandment includes all slaves, not only Israelites but also "strangers." It is based, no doubt, on a certain view of physical and spiritual needs but also on the memory of the degraded character of "rigorous" slavery. Alienated work and humiliation do capture at least part of the oppressiveness of Egyptian bondage.

One might, alternatively, understand *be-farech* in the sense of physical cruelty. Here, too, the laws proclaimed immediately after the escape from Egypt, where the Israelites had been beaten and killed, seem designed to rule out Egyptian oppression: "And if a man smite his servant or his maid . . . and he die under his hand; he shall surely be punished" (Exod. 21:20). Slave-owners who kill their slaves are not "put to death," as in the case of ordinary murder (see 21:12), so this isn't quite what Ephraim Urbach calls it: the "absolute equality of slave and free man in all matters regarding the judicial safeguarding of their lives. . . . " Still, the safeguards established by the Exodus prohibitions have "no parallel in either Greek or Roman law."[14] Moreover, if a slave suffered physical injury at the hands of his master, he was to be set free (21:26–27). Again, we don't know if these laws were enforced, or how consistently they were enforced, during different periods of Israel's history. But they are Exodus laws, and they presumably express the Israelite understanding of their own suffering in Egypt.

It was also part of the oppressiveness of Egyptian slavery that the Israelites were not, in their own view, legitimately slaves at all. They had not been captured in war, and they had never sold themselves into bondage. They were, as I have said, a guest people, and then they were guest workers. This was the injustice committed by the Egyptians, according to the philosopher Philo: they made slaves "of men who were not only free but guests [and] suppliants. . . . "[15] An old legend, retold in the Midrash, has it that the Israelites were at first paid wages for their work on the store cities Pithom and Raamses. Then the wages were withheld, and they were simply forced to work.[16] This experience—some dim memory of it or some story about it elaborated over the years—seems to lie behind the Deuteronomic law of wages:

> Thou shalt not oppress an hired servant that is poor and needy, whether he be of thy brethren or of thy strangers that are in thy land. . . . At his day thou shalt give him his hire, neither shall the sun go down upon it. [And then, after two more commandments:] For thou shalt remember that thou wast a bondsman in Egypt. (25:14–15, 18)

The law is given in the singular, but it is a crucial part of the experience of the Israelites in Egypt that they were not enslaved one by one, but all together. They were made "poor and needy" because they were strangers in the land.

Dependent upon political protection, they found themselves helpless when protection was suddenly withdrawn. They were not the victims of the market but of the state, the absolute monarchy of the pharaohs. Hence, Samuel's warning to the elders of Israel against choosing a king, which is surely meant to recall the Exodus experience: "And he shall take . . . your goodliest young men . . . and put them to work . . . and ye shall be his servants" (1 Sam. 8:16–17). Under an absolute king, it might be said, the whole body of subjects are like strangers in Egypt.

Egyptian bondage was the bondage of a people to the arbitrary power of the state. Chattel slavery was conceivably preferable, for it was a condition governed by legal norms. In "the house of slaves," there were no norms. The Israelites were submitted to a bondage without limit— without rest, without recompense, without restraint, without a purpose they they might make their own. In Egypt, slavery was a kind of political rule. Of course, Pharaoh profited from the work of his Israelite slaves, but he did not enslave them for the sake of the profit. The slaves were exploited, as all slaves are, but it is more important in the biblical account that they were oppressed, that is, ruled with cruelty, ruled tyrannically. The Exodus tradition speaks against tyranny—and that is the way it figures, for example, in the preaching of Savonarola, in the pamphlets of John Milton, and in American revolutionary sermons attacking the "British Pharaoh."[17]

The form of the tyranny, of course, was hard labor, and so the story invites, again, a social and economic translation. The neat line that Hannah Arendt draws, in her book on revolution, between the political question and the social question, between tyranny and misery, cannot be drawn here.[18] The Exodus story seems to encompass both. In applications of the story, the people of Israel are readily compared to an oppressed class. A pamphlet by the Leveller John Lilburne, published in London in 1645, suggests that this sort of thing isn't only a modern reading or misreading of the text.

> But some will say, that our bondage is not yet so bad as that of Egypt was, for all the Jews were in great bondage under the Egyptians, and yet many of ours are exempted; unto that I yield, and do confess that few of our great and mighty men do either work the clay or make the bricks; but they lay either all or most part of the burden on the poor by heavy labor. . . .[19]

The Deuteronomic command about the "poor and needy" makes a similar point: like Lilburne's England, the promised land breeds its own oppressors—"*our* great and mighty men." One doesn't need Egyptians. But the biblical writers attempt no extended social reference. The only groups that the text knows are ethnic and political in character, and the Exodus is first of all an account of the oppression of such a group by a savage ruler in a foreign land. That's why the memory of the Exodus is more often invoked on behalf of aliens than on behalf of slaves: "Thou shalt not oppress a stranger: for ye know the heart [*nefesh:* "spirit" or "feelings"] of a stranger, seeing ye were strangers in the land of Egypt" (Exod. 23:9). It is easy to understand why the Exodus story appealed so much to African slaves in the American South. Though these were chattel slaves, they were also aware of themselves as a separate people, strangers in a strange land, who shared a common fate. Egyptian bondage is paradigmatic for abolitionist politics, and for radical politics generally, be-

radical political femin...

cause of its collective character. It invites a collective response—not manumission, the common goal of Greek and Roman slaves, but liberation.

We can think of the Exodus as an example of what is today called "national liberation." The people as a whole are enslaved, and then the people as a whole are delivered. At the same time, however, the uses of the story in Israel's own history—first in legislation and then in prophecy— suggest that the Egyptian model reaches to every sort of oppression and to every sort of liberation. Perhaps the crucial point is the linking of oppression and state power: "the oppression in Egypt," as Croatto says, "is of a *political* order . . . [it is] exercised from the seat of political power."[20] Hence the escape from bondage is also the defeat of a tyrant—and the escape is only possible because of the defeat. Tyranny is symbolized by Pharaoh's horses and chariots, the core of his army and the source of his power (the symbolism recurs throughout the Bible).[21] The overlord of the house of slaves is also an arrogant warlord, and so he is presented in the song of triumph that the Israelites sing on the far side of the Red Sea:

> The enemy said, I will pursue, I will overtake, I will divide the spoil, my lust shall be satisfied upon them; I will draw my sword, my hand shall destroy them.   (Exod. 15:9)

But God is a greater warrior, and the tyrant is defeated: "the horse and his rider hath he thrown into the sea." This was the moment of liberation. Benjamin Franklin's proposal for the Great Seal captures the political sense of the Exodus text. Franklin went beyond the text, however, with his proposed inscription: "Resistance to tyrants is obedience to God." In Exodus history, for reasons I will explore in the next chapter, the Israelites do not themselves fight against Pharaoh. It is God alone who destroys the Egyptian chariots. The call to resist tyrants is nevertheless a characteristic reading of the text—a matter not of obeying God, precisely, but of imitating Him.

III

BONDAGE and oppression are the key ideas in the Exodus story, but the analysis of these ideas does not exhaust the significance of Egypt. No old regime is merely oppressive; it is attractive, too, else the escape from it would be much easier than it is. The attractions of Egypt don't appear very plainly in the text, but they figure necessarily in the interpretation of the text, that is, in efforts to expand upon and explain the foreshortened, often enigmatic narrative. We can best begin, though, with a well-known passage from chapter 16 of the Book of Exodus. The Israelites have been in the wilderness now for forty-five days.

> And the whole congregation of the children of Israel murmured against Moses and Aaron. . . . And the children of Israel said unto them, would to God we had died by the hand of the Lord in the land of Egypt, when we sat by the fleshpots and when we did eat bread to the full. . . . (16:2–3)

I first read this passage years ago, when I was very young, and focused then, as I shall do now, on that wonderful word "fleshpots." My attention was drawn, I confess, rather to the first part of the word than to the second; in fact, I don't remember thinking about the second at all. Nor did I ever firmly grasp, until I began working on this book, just what a fleshpot was. A prosaic object, a pot for cooking meat: even in the United States today, we sit, or most of us do, by our fleshpots. But my adolescent preoccupation with the flesh was on the mark, for meat throughout most of human history has been the food of the privileged, and "fleshpots," in the plural, doesn't refer to a lot of pots but to luxuries and sensual delights. I don't know whether the word had this meaning for the authors and editors of the Book of Exodus, or whether it came to have this meaning because of the use they made of it.[22] In either case, we can say that the house of bondage, in the eyes of its erstwhile inhabitants, was also a land of luxury.

This became the standard view—so that generations of reformers have railed against Egyptian luxuries. Ernst Bloch takes the luxuries to be outsized and tawdry, the mirror image of modern consumer culture: "Mammoth Egypt . . . the shoddy product and symbol of the world that has come to be."[23] In the eyes of Savonarola, Florentine "vanities" simply repeated Egyptian luxuries. Preaching on Exodus, he stressed the rich and lascivious life of the Egyptians; the promised land, the new society, would be different.[24] The Jewish historical and interpretive literature takes a similar line. One rabbinic commentary argues, against the apparent meaning of the text, that when Pharaoh issued his command to the midwives, he was "as much interested in preserving the female children as in bringing about the death of the male children. [The Egyptians] were very sensual, and were desirous of having as many women as possible at their service."[25] Josephus writes in the same vein in his *Antiquities of the Jews:* "The Egyptians are a nation addicted unto delicacy and impatient of labor, subject only to their pleasures. . . ."[26] In these passages, we can hear the note of disapproval that is missing in the people's complaint about the fleshpots (though not, of course, in the narrator's report of the complaint or in Moses' reply: "Your murmurings are not against us but against the Lord"). The note of disapproval is sounded much more strongly in Leviticus and Deuteronomy and then by the Prophets. "After the doings of the land of Egypt, wherein ye dwelt, shall ye not do" (Lev. 18:3). Early Judaism is defined by its rejection not only of Egyptian bondage but also of Egyptian culture: the customary ways of the upper classes as they ate and drank, dressed and housed themselves, amused themselves, worshipped their gods, and buried their dead.

The Israelite rejection of luxury is commonly described as the response of nomads to an urban civilization.[27] So it must have been, at least in part. A certain sort of desert puritanism survived for many centuries even after the Israelites were settled in the promised land. Thus the sect called the Rechabites, on whose doctrine Jeremiah reports:

> We will drink no wine, for Jonadab, the son of Rechab our father commanded us, saying, Ye shall drink no wine, neither ye, nor your sons forever. Neither shall ye build houses, nor sow seed, nor plant vineyards, nor have any: but all your days ye shall dwell in tents . . .   (35:6–7)

Presumably the Rechabites ate meat—the daily manna had long since ceased—but they rejected the luxuries of urban life, and they did so from a resolutely nomadic standpoint. They were loyal to the God who spurned David's offer to build a temple: "Shalt thou build me an house for me to dwell in? Whereas I have not dwelt in any house since the time that I brought up the children of Israel out of Egypt . . . but have walked in a tent and in a tabernacle" (2 Sam. 7:5–6).

But the example of the Rechabites is not definitive for the people as a whole, who did not dream of austerity but of milk and honey. To be sure, when the Israelites celebrated their deliverance in later years, they ate matzo, "the bread of affliction," slave bread, and the eating expresses (according to a modern commentary on the Hagaddah, the prayerbook for the family observance of the Passover) "the avoidance of indulgence and arrogance . . . the simple and unspoiled life of a servant of God."[28] But they ate the matzo, as Jews still do today, at a festive banquet, reclining on cushions, drinking wine. They "remembered" the experience of oppression while enjoying the pleasures of freedom. Nor did freedom require that they live in tents, moving with the seasons.

Desert puritanism is not a sufficient explanation for the refusal of Egyptian culture. The refusal, here and with all latter-day puritanisms, too, has to do with the complex attitude that the oppressed take toward the culture of their oppressors. The Israelites in Egypt were attracted by Egyptian life and by Egyptian worship, but in neither of these could they fully or freely share. We might think again about Exodus 16: "It does not say," as the Midrash reports, " 'when we did eat *from* the flesh pots,' but 'when we sat *by* the flesh pots.' They had to eat their bread without meat."[29] They smelled the meat, but didn't taste it, and what they longed for in the desert was their longing in the house of bondage. But surely this kind of longing is always mixed with resentment and anger. Or, better, if some of the Israelites wanted, as the Midrash also reports, "to be like the Egyptians," others, with more pride, wanted to stress their differences and turn their backs on Egyptian "delicacies."[30]

The commentaries are full of stories of Israelite assimilation in Egypt. "The people of Israel," said Savonarola, "became half-Egyptian. . . ."[31] Centuries earlier, the rabbis had suggested that many Israelites dressed like Egyptians and adopted Egyptian names. They begot "strange children," reports one midrashic account, following a passage in the prophet Hosea (5:7) that is taken to mean, "they abolished the covenant of circumcision." A later Midrash, written when knowledge of Egyptian culture had long faded, interprets the line "And the land was filled with them" (Exod. 1:7) to indicate that "the amphitheaters and circuses were full of them."[32] But the story of the bondage years is also told in an entirely different way. Some of the rabbis argued, for example, that there existed a covenant among the Israelites, years before Sinai, to preserve their ancestral customs and the memory of the God of the patriarchs. No Jew, one of them said, ever broke faith with the community of Jewish slaves in Egypt.[33] (Who was it then who informed Pharaoh about Moses' killing of the taskmaster?) These versions of the Egyptian experience seem contradictory, but perhaps they describe different aspects of the same history. Egypt was a center of wealth and good living; it makes sense to suggest that many Israelites admired the very people who oppressed them, copied Egyptian ways, curried Egyptian favor. And other Israelites feared and repressed the impulse to act similarly in themselves.

One can trace the same tension in religious practice. The worship of idols is undoubtedly the most important of the "doings of the land of Egypt" that the Israelites were warned not to do. It is an old tradition that in Egypt they were idol worshippers, slaves imitating the religion of their masters (and not finding in it, as black slaves found in Christianity, a gospel of freedom). Ezekiel elaborates on the flat assertion of Joshua 24 that the Israelites served strange gods "beyond the river and in Egypt."

And they committed whoredoms in Egypt; they committed whoredoms in their youth: there were their breasts pressed, and there they bruised the teats of their virginity. . . . (23:3)

And then the prophet threatens the people with destruction because they have brought their whoredoms with them out of Egypt into the promised land, because they have continued to go "whoring after the heathen" and because they are "polluted with their idols." The language here is the language of sexual disgust. It is most explicit in another passage from Ezekiel, describing Israel as a woman who remembers

the days of her youth, wherein she played the harlot in the land of Egypt. For she doted upon their paramours, whose flesh is as the flesh of asses, and whose issue is as the issue of horses. (23:19–20)

This is the wrong way to remember the house of bondage, but it recalls accurately enough, perhaps, the animal gods of Egypt. Or, it refers to orgiastic forms of worship more commonly associated with the gods of Canaan. Or, it may be nothing more than a standard metaphorical reference for idol worship generally. In any case, Ezekiel can serve as a text on the sensual appeal of idolatry and the moral revulsion against it. The prophet expresses the revulsion, but recognizes the appeal: "for she doted upon their paramours." In the episode of the golden calf, which I will deal with at some length in the next chapter, it is Aaron who recognizes the appeal (and perhaps succumbs to it) and Moses who expresses and then acts out the revulsion. But it is only the two together that give us Egypt through Israelite eyes.[34]

The Israelites saw what came, later on, to be called

decadence, a high culture that had gotten too high: over-ripe, tainted, corrupt and, at the same time, rich and alluring. In an extraordinary piece of intellectual play (in Exod. 15 and Deut. 7), the plagues with which God punished the Egyptians are turned into Egyptian diseases and made emblematic of the corruption of the land—so that going back to Egypt means, among other things, to experience the "evil diseases of Egypt."[35] This is the way Egypt most often figures in later revolutionary literature. A sermon by the Puritan preacher Stephen Marshall before the House of Commons in 1640 provides a typical example: "Egypt was never more bespread with locusts and frogs than our kingdom is with horrible profaneness, uncleanness, oppression, deceit, and whatsoever is a stench in the Lord's nostrils." The stench comes, I would guess, from Exodus 7, where the waters of the Nile are turned into blood: "And the river stank." What stinks in Marshall's nostrils are popish ceremonies and the rule of bishops. But we need to round out Marshall's argument with the words of another Puritan minister, who commented sadly on "the natural popery of the multitude, and of our own hearts."[36]

One might say of the Israelites that they were natural (naturalized) Egyptians as well as rebels against Egyptian bondage and corruption. Indeed, the promised land, the opposite of bondage and corruption, is not quite as different from Egypt as I earlier suggested it was. This last point is quite deliberately conveyed in one of the more remarkable passages of the Exodus story, which describes the rebellion against Moses organized by the tribal leaders Dathan and Abiram. "Is it a small thing," these two are reported as asking, "that thou hast brought us up out of a land that floweth with milk and honey, to kill us in the wilderness? . . . " (Num. 16:13). Egypt was, of course, a

[handwritten margin note top: Exodus from a culture of luxury that common people can't partake of]

land of milk and honey, and the slaves knew that it was, even if they couldn't, or even if they wouldn't, savor its delights. And the divine promise was shaped to their consciousness—milk and honey of their own, milk and honey without the evil diseases of the Egyptians. The promised land repeats the affluence of the house of bondage, but this is supposed to be an affluence more widely shared than it was in Egypt, and it is supposed to be an affluence that doesn't corrupt. And when it isn't shared, and does corrupt, then it is time to invoke again the Exodus story.

[handwritten margin note: shared this affluence?]

Without the new ideas of oppression and corruption, without the sense of injustice, without moral revulsion, neither Exodus nor revolution would be possible. In the text as we have it, the new ideas are shadowed by their older opposites: the sense of injustice by resignation, revulsion by longing. The shadows are sharply drawn; this is part of the realism of the biblical story. But it is the new ideas that make the new event. They provide the energy of the Exodus, and they define its direction. The direction is definitive not only for the deliverance of Israel but for all later interpretations and applications of that deliverance. Henceforth, any move toward Egypt is a "going back" in moral time and space. When Milton wrote of the English in 1660 that they were "choosing them a captain back for Egypt," he did not mean to describe a mere return (or a cyclical repetition) but a retrogression, a "backsliding" to bondage and corruption.[37] The slide is not incomprehensible, for Egypt is a complex reality. But it is a defeat. It is the paradigm of revolutionary defeat.

TWO

The Murmurings:

Slaves in the Wilderness

IN a poem dedicated to Joseph Brodsky, playing on the story of the biblical Joseph, Anthony Hecht has a lovely line about "Egypt . . . that old school of the soul."[1] The idea of Egypt as a school, or at least a kind of training ground, is fairly common in the Exodus literature. Alternatively, Egypt is a furnace, the "iron furnace" of Deuteronomy 4:20, which the rabbis explain as a cauldron for refining precious metals: what emerges, presumably, is pure gold. This is an optimistic view of the effects of oppression on ordinary men and women. Many years later, Savonarola took the same view, expounding the text "But the more they afflicted them, the more they multiplied and grew" (Exod. 1:12)—and thinking, I suppose, of the Florentine people under the rule of the Medicis. The Israelites, Savonarola explained, multiplied in numbers and grew in spirit. He went on in his next sermon to talk enthusiastically about Moses' killing of the Egyptian taskmaster, an example of spiritedness, certainly, but not of a spiritedness bred by affliction.[2] For Moses had grown up in Pharaoh's court and never worked with brick and mortar (he had probably never worked at all). We can find a more realistic account of what was learned in "that old school of the soul" in a rabbinic interpretation of the killing of the taskmaster. Recall the text:

> And it came to pass . . . when Moses was grown, that he went out unto his brethren, and looked on their burdens: and he spied an Egyptian smiting an Hebrew, one of his brethren. And he looked this way and that way, and when he saw that there was no man, he slew the Egyptian, and hid him in the sand.   (Exod. 2:11–12)

We might think that Moses simply wanted to make sure that he was not seen; killing a taskmaster would be a serious crime in the house of bondage. But the prophet Isaiah takes a different view in a description of divine justice that obviously echoes the Exodus text. Isaiah imagines God looking down on the evil in the world and on the sins of Israel and waiting for, looking for, some human response:

> And he saw that there was no man, and he wondered that there was no intercessor: therefore his arm brought salvation unto [Israel]; and his righteousness, it sustained him. (59:16)

Building on these lines, some of the rabbis argued that when Moses looked this way and that way, he was looking for an Israelite ready to intercede and defend the beaten slave; he was looking for a *real* man, a proud and rebellious spirit. And when he saw no sign of resistance, when he saw, according to a midrashic commentator, "that there was no one ready to champion the cause of the Holy One Blessed be He," he acted himself, hoping to arouse his

44

people and to "straighten their backs." This interpretation is the source, we are told, of the maxim attributed to Hillel: "Where there is no man, try to be one."[3] (I should note that the word "man" is used here in the generic sense, for among the few men in the Exodus story are two women, the midwives of Exodus 1, who refuse Pharaoh's order to kill the newborn sons of the Israelites.)

women

What the bulk of the slaves learned in Egypt was servitude and slavishness. They learned, as I argued in the last chapter, to imitate their masters, but only at a distance, in their longings, fearfully; they admitted into their souls the degradation of slavery. This is a possible meaning of the line, "there was no man," and it is one of the major themes of the Exodus story and of the early and late interpretive literature. I shall work through a few characteristic passages before coming to the key passage, Exodus 32, the story of the golden calf. I want to suggest that there exists in the text an argument about the moral and psychological effects of oppression. The argument is remarkably like that of Stanley Elkins, in his well-known and highly controversial book about slavery in the American South.[4] Indeed, Elkins would have done well to cite the Exodus rather than relying for his comparative material on the more extreme case of the Holocaust: for the South was more like a house of bondage than a death camp. There is, in any case, a long history of citation in which the slavishness of the Israelites is used to explain, first, the forty years of wandering in the desert and the reiterated attempts to return to Egypt and then, later on, the difficulties of revolutionary or liberationist politics.

I will begin with a story that has only the skimpiest of textual foundations, but that provides insight nonetheless into the realities of Exodus politics. When God, speaking out of the burning bush, commands Moses to return to

45

Egypt, He tells him to gather the elders of Israel and go with them to confront Pharaoh (Exod. 3:18). And Moses and Aaron do gather the elders and tell them of the coming deliverance. But when they speak to Pharaoh, they appear to be alone: "And afterward Moses and Aaron went in, and told Pharaoh, thus saith the Lord God of Israel, Let my people go . . ." (Exod. 5:1). What happened to the elders? This is the midrashic account:

> Our rabbis said: the elders went along at the beginning but stealthily slipped away, one by one, two by two, and disappeared. By the time [Moses and Aaron] reached Pharaoh's palace, not one of them remained. This is witnessed by the text, "And afterward Moses and Aaron went in." But where were the elders? They had slipped away.[5]

They slipped away, says Rashi, "because they were afraid."[6] These words are probably meant to recall Exodus 14:10, where the Israelites find themselves trapped between the Egyptian army and the sea: "And when Pharaoh drew nigh, the children of Israel lifted up their eyes and, behold, the Egyptians marched after them, and they were sore afraid. . . ." As the elders, so the people as a whole: all the Israelites were afraid of their masters, unwilling to challenge Pharaoh in his palace, overawed by the sight of his army. According to the biblical account, there were six hundred thousand men in the Israelite tribes that marched out of Egypt. Why should such a large number, asks the medieval commentator Abraham Ibn Ezra, stand in fear of their lives? Why didn't they turn and fight? They were psychologically incapable, he says; they suffered from a slave mentality; for centuries they had not defended themselves—not, at least, by fighting.[7] Indeed, they were the very opposite of spirited men. Thus Exodus 6:9: "They harkened not unto Moses for anguish of spirit

46

and for cruel bondage." The Hebrew is *kotzer ruach,* literally "shortness of spirit," an idiom for impatience, but here, I think, meant literally: "dispiritedness."

The Book of Exodus describes a people weighed down by oppression, crushed, frightened, subservient, despondent. The same description is applied again and again by later reformers and revolutionaries complaining about the unwillingness of their own people to rise up against tyranny. Even Savonarola, who argued, as we have seen, that oppression only strengthened the Israelite spirit, could not always resist the complaint. "Anguish of spirit" is pusillanimousness, he said in the seventeenth of his Exodus sermons, and it is a Florentine as well as an Israelite condition: "You do to me what the Israelites did to Moses . . . ."[8] That means, you don't hearken to my words or follow me when I confront the tyrant. Preaching in Plymouth in 1774, an American minister was even more pessimistic: "deprived of liberty," he argued, "oppressed and enslaved men . . . become stupid, and debased in spirit, indolent and groveling, indifferent to all valuable improvement and hardly capable of any."[9] On this view, the revolutionary struggle that had already begun was literally impossible. But oppression in the American colonies (at least British oppression, as distinct from the local oppression of slaves and indentured servants) seems mostly notional: a very distant tyranny. The idea of "dispiritedness and cruel bondage" has more force, I think, in Latin America today. Croatto has a long list of concrete cases, in which he "rediscovers" the meaning of Exodus oppression: the slaves internalize their own "crushed identity."[10]

Conceivably, the Israelite slaves in Egypt learned to have compassion for others in a similar plight. This is a contemporary rabbi's interpretation of the school and furnace metaphors: "Egyptian bondage served to implant within us the quality of kindness. . . ."[11] That may be so; but it did not implant the qualities of initiative, self-respect, anger at oppression, militancy. Those qualities are carried in the earlier parts of the Exodus story by Moses and, of course, by God Himself. But I don't want to exaggerate this point, for there is some textual evidence that the Israelites were politically divided, and a folkloric account of that moment at the sea (elaborated in numerous stories and poems) holds that only some of the people were "sore afraid" and eager to return to bondage, while others were ready to fight, and still others plunged into the sea even before the waters had parted, so confident were they of divine assistance.[12] The very fact that the slaves in Egypt "cry out" to God suggests, as Croatto goes on to say, that "they had not wholly internalized the state of oppression."[13] They still possessed some idea of themselves as free or potentially free men and women. The picture of a people deprived of that idea, radically dispirited and degraded, invites a revolutionary politics in which oppressed men and women are treated with the same contempt by their liberators as by their oppressors. Hegel sets the stage for this kind of politics with a contemptuous dismissal of the Jewish people in his *Spirit of Christianity:*

> For the Jews a great thing was done, but they [did] not inaugurate it with heroic deeds of their own. . . . The Jews vanquish, but they have not battled. . . . It is no wonder that this nation, which in its emancipation bore the most slavelike demeanor, regretted leaving Egypt.[14]

One could, in fact, make a similar argument about most of the great revolutionary deliverances. For the English in 1640, and the French in 1789, and the Russians in 1917, it is also the case that "a great thing was done." The old

48

regime was gravely weakened or actually brought down by external forces, not by an internal and heroic resistance. Revolutionary politics, in its full sense, begins only after the collapse or near collapse of state power. But we cannot conclude from this that oppressed men and women have nothing at all to do with their own liberation.

Theorists of revolution (and writers about the Exodus) can usefully be divided into two groups: those who believe that the liberation of the oppressed will always be like that of Hegel's Jews, a gift of God (or of history or the vanguard); and those who believe that liberation must to some degree, at least, be the work of the oppressed themselves. Among Jewish writers, for obvious reasons, there was always some resistance to arguments like Hegel's—even if this meant denying that Israel's deliverance was entirely the work of God's mighty hand. In any case, Hegel's view is unrealistic, for if God were wholly responsible, the people could never have held back, as we know they did; and if they were able to hold back, then they were also able to step forward.

> Rabbi Eliezer said: This reflects great credit on Israel. For when Moses said to them: "Arise and go forth," they did not say, How can we go forth into the wilderness when we have no sustenance for the way? But they had faith and went.[15]

II

BUT the biblical text never underestimates popular fearfulness, and that is its great strength. We get no sense from the text of what forms fearfulness took during the long years of bondage. The history of those years is too quickly told. And so there is nothing in Jewish literature quite like the Sambo figure described by Elkins, the slave who panders to his masters, who is abject, childish, irresponsible. Presumably there were Israelites like that in Egypt; perhaps we will one day find them described in Egyptian literature. The Jews produce another stereotype, the "murmurer," whom we might think of as Sambo in the wilderness: not someone who is adjusted to his slavery but someone who complains endlessly about his liberation.

There are many "murmurings," but we will do best to consider a passage that I have already referred to, Exodus 16:2–3:

> And the whole congregation of the children of Israel murmured against Moses and Aaron in the wilderness. And the children of Israel said unto them, would to God we had died by the hand of the Lord in the land of Egypt, when we sat by the fleshpots and when we did eat bread to the full; for ye have brought us forth into this wilderness to kill this whole assembly with hunger.

The miracle of the manna follows, and God, were He not omniscient, might plausibly have assumed that the people would henceforth be content. He had brought them out of bondage, opened the sea for them, destroyed Pharaoh's army, and sustained them in the wilderness—and that should have been enough. But it wasn't enough: manna in the wilderness bred a nostalgia for meat in the house of bondage, and in the Book of Numbers the complaint is renewed:

> Who shall give us flesh to eat? We remember the fish which we did eat in Egypt freely; the cucumbers, and the

melons, and the leeks, and the onions, and the garlic: But now our soul is dried away; there is nothing at all beside this manna before our eyes. (11:4–6)

The murmuring in these two passages reflects, I suppose, the normal anxiety of men and women faced with the difficulties of the march, the terrible austerity of the desert. God and Moses take the long view, see the promised land ahead, and think that no hardship is too great to endure for the sake of such an end. But the people, or many of them, were unsure of the end and thought that the real test of divine power and solicitude was more immediate: "Can God furnish a table in the wilderness?" (Psalms 78:19). Pharaoh at least fed his slaves, and he fed them, so they remembered or misremembered, abundantly. The conflict, then, is between the materialism of the people and the idealism of their leaders, or it is between the demands of the present moment and the promise of the future. These are common political formulations, and one can find them developed in a great variety of ways in the rabbinic literature, usually, but not always, in ways unsympathetic to the people and the present moment. The same argument appears later on too. In one of the most important sermons of the English Revolution, preached to the House of Commons on the day after the execution of Charles I, John Owen castigated the English as a people unable to focus on "their approaching liberty," demanding instead that the new government provide instant relief:

Do [the people] lack drink?—Moses is the cause. Do they lack meat?—this Moses would starve them. He would not let them alone by the fleshpots of Egypt; for this they are ready to stone him. At this day, have we too much rain, or too short a harvest?—it is laid on the shoulders of the present government.[16]

The same theme is struck by a preacher in New Haven in 1777:

. . . How soon does our faith fail us, and we begin to murmur against Moses and Aaron and wish ourselves back again in Egypt where we had some comforts of life, which we are now deprived of?—not considering that . . . in any deliverance there are great troubles and difficulties. . . .[17]

But this is too simple an account of the murmurings, for what is at issue is not only the difficulty but the very meaning of deliverance—indeed of liberty itself. The rabbis approach this issue through an elaborate interpretation of the sentence about "the fish that we did eat in Egypt freely." This apparently means free of charge; Pharaoh is said to have reasoned thusly: "How could [the slaves] work hard and attain good results on an empty stomach?" And so he fed them. Modern commentators cite a passage from Herodotus, who claims to have read an inscription on one of the pyramids reporting that sixteen hundred measures of garlic and onions were provided for the workmen.[18] But some rabbis insisted that "freely" meant "free from commandments." For the wilderness wasn't only a world of austerity; it was also a world of laws—the whole legal system founded by Moses, the dietary code, the prohibition of cooking on the Sabbath, and so on. Manna itself had come with rules and regulations "that I may prove them," God said, "whether they will walk in my law, or no" (Exod. 16:4). It was against all this that the people rebelled, remembering Egypt now as a house of freedom.[19]

Indeed, there is a kind of freedom in bondage: it is one

of the oldest themes in political thought, prominent especially in classical and neoclassical republicanism and in
Calvinist Christianity, that tyranny and license go together. The childish and irresponsible slave or subject is
free in ways the republican citizen and Protestant saint
can never be. And there is a kind of bondage in freedom:
the bondage of law, obligation, and responsibility. True
freedom, in the rabbinic view, lies in servitude to God.
The Israelites had been Pharaoh's slaves; in the wilderness
they became God's servants—the Hebrew word is the
same; and once they agree to God's rule, He and Moses,
His deputy, force them to be free. This, according to
Rousseau, was Moses' great achievement; he transformed
a herd of "wretched fugitives," who lacked both virtue
and courage, into "a free people." He didn't do this merely
by breaking their chains but also by organizing them into
a "political society" and giving them laws.[20] He brought
them what is currently called "positive freedom," that is,
not so much (not at all!) a way of life free from regulation
but rather a way of life to whose regulation they could,
and did, agree. That this latter condition is properly called
freedom is an idea much criticized in recent philosophical
literature, and sometimes rightly, but it contains a deep
truth nonetheless about the process of liberation. The
Israelite slaves could become free only insofar as they
accepted the discipline of freedom, the obligation to live
up to a common standard and to take responsibility for
their own actions. They did accept a common standard:
hence the Sinai covenant (the subject of chapter 3); but
they also resented the standard and feared the responsibility it entailed. They had what we can think of as an
Egyptian idea of freedom.

And so the wilderness had to be a new school of the
soul. That is why the Israelites had to spend such a long

time in the wilderness. They did not march by the most direct route from Egypt to Canaan; instead God led them by an indirect route. In his *Guide of the Perplexed,* Maimonides explains the indirection. "For a sudden transition from one opposite to another is impossible . . . it is not in the nature of man that, after having been brought up in slavish service . . . he should all of a sudden wash off from his hands the dirt [of slavery]." Characteristically, Maimonides acknowledges the difficulties of liberation and is prepared to deal gently with the Israelite murmurers—and he conceives God in his own image: "the deity uses a gracious ruse," he writes, "in causing [the people] to wander perplexedly in the desert until their souls became courageous . . . and until, moreover, people were born who were not accustomed to humiliation and servitude."[21] As Nehama Leibowitz has suggested, this is a rabbinic formula for the Fabian "inevitability of gradualness."[22] With shameless anachronism, I will describe it as the social democratic version of the Exodus. It is curiously and surely unconsciously echoed by Karl Marx, writing about the aftermath of 1848:

> The revolution, which finds here not its end, but its organizational beginning, is no short-lived revolution. The present generation is like the Jews whom Moses led through the wilderness. It has not only a new world to conquer, it must go under in order to make room for men who are able to cope with a new world.[23]

Maimonides writes of those who will be born, Marx, more harshly, of those who have to die. Neither one says anything in these passages about the large number of Israelites who will be killed. But there is violence in the wilderness, not only marching and murmuring, but fighting too, internal war and divine punishment. We won't get to the end of the problems posed by slavishness and liberation until we look closely at the incident of the golden calf, where the murmuring of the people turned into something like a counterrevolution—and where the murmurers were dealt with by methods very different from Maimonides' "gracious ruse."

III

READERS of this book probably know more about the golden calf than they think they do. But I will briefly retell the story. Moses has been on the mountaintop now for forty days, and the people are anxious and frightened by his absence. Or rather, some of them are anxious and frightened: one has to add the qualification for the text makes it clear later on that the people at the foot of the mountain were not of one mind. "Distrust overwhelmed a section of this great people," as Judah Halevi writes in his *Kuzari*, "and they began to divide into parties and factions. . . ."[24] One of these parties approaches Aaron, Moses' brother, and demands that he make them an idol, a visible god. Aaron weakly complies, collecting their golden jewelry and shaping the molten metal into a calf —or, perhaps better, a young bull. The people worship the idol, feasting and "playing" in front of it. The Hebrew word for "to play," *litzachek,* has, according to Rashi, sexual connotations: the worship was orgiastic.[25] God, in a rage, tells Moses what is happening down below and proposes to destroy the people whom He has just delivered and make of Moses' line a "great nation." But Moses argues with God and wins his promise of ultimate forgiveness. Then Moses comes down the mountain carrying the tablets, enters the camp, sees the people (or some of them) worshipping the idol, and is as angry as God was when He saw the same thing. Moses smashes the tablets and mobilizes his supporters:

Who is on the Lord's side? Let him come unto me. And all the sons of Levi gathered themselves together unto him. And he said unto them, Thus saith the Lord God of Israel, put every man his sword by his side, and go in and out from gate to gate throughout the camp, and slay every man his brother, and every man his companion, and every man his neighbor. And the children of Levi did according to the word of Moses: and there fell of the people that day about three thousand men. (Exod. 32:26–28)

There are many things to talk about here, and a vast interpretive and critical literature to review. I shall focus on only a few central themes. First, the golden calf itself. Some contemporary scholars argue that the idol is of Canaanite origin and that the whole story is a late interpolation, a piece of propaganda aimed at the northern kingdom of Israel, where an altar of golden bulls was set up during the reign of King Jeroboam.[26] But the Egyptians also worshipped a bull god, Apis, and the story loses much of its meaning if it is lifted out of the Exodus context; at least, it loses the meaning it has had within the several traditions to which I am committed: the Jewish account of deliverance and the political theory of liberation. So I shall follow the philosopher Philo who says, in his *Life of Moses*, that the people "fashioned a golden bull, in imitation of the animal held most sacred in [Egypt]"; and I shall follow the Puritan preacher who wrote in 1643: "out of Egyptian jewels, they made an Egyptian idol . . . they intended to return for Egypt"; and I shall follow

Lincoln Steffens, in our own century: "the children of Israel were going back to their old gods, the gods of the Egyptians."[27] This is the great crisis of the Exodus.

Rabbinic interpreters stress the link between the golden calf and the years in Egypt at another point in the story: when Moses argues with God on behalf of the people. The textual account of the argument is brief and not wholly satisfying. Moses seems to score a debater's point: what will the Egyptians say, he asks, if You destroy a people whom they merely enslaved? The rabbis tried to imagine Moses defending the people in some more positive way. But what claim could he make on their behalf? Surely their crime was great. They had only just made their covenant with God and sworn obedience: "All that the Lord hath spoken will we do and obey" (Exod. 24:7). And now they have "corrupted themselves" with idol worship. What could Moses say? The question was of especial importance in the first centuries of the common era, for Christian polemicists used the story of the golden calf to argue that though the Jews had once been elected of God, they had almost immediately rejected the election, themselves had refused to be God's chosen people.[28] Here is one midrashic response:

Rabbi Huna said: It can be compared to a wise man who opened a perfumery shop for his son in a street frequented by prostitutes. The street did its work, the business also did its share; and the boy's youth contributed its part, with the result that he fell into evil ways. When his father came and caught him with a prostitute, he began to shout: "I'll kill you." But his friend who was there said: "You ruined this youth's character and yet you shout at him! You ignored all other professions and taught him only to be a perfumer, you foresook all other districts and opened a shop for him just in a street where prostitutes dwell!" This is that Moses said: "Lord of the Universe! You ignored the entire world and caused Your children to be enslaved only in Egypt, where all worshipped [idols], from whom Your children learned [to do corruptly]. It is for this reason that they have made a Calf! . . . bear in mind whence You have brought them forth!"[29]

It is all God's fault—which is not to say that He (directly) caused the people to worship idols but that He should have foreseen the consequences of Egyptian bondage; He should understand—if He can't, who can?—the nature of historical determination. Oppression is an experience with necessary effects, and God, confronting those effects, should not now be impatient (or dispirited). Here again is the argument for gradualism. Physically, the escape from Egypt is sudden, glorious, complete; spiritually and politically, it is very slow, a matter of two steps forward, one step back. I want to stress that this is a lesson drawn from the Exodus experience again and again. A newly freed slave in America in 1862, writing to his fellows, provides a nice example: "There must be no looking back to Egypt. Israel passed forty years in the wilderness. . . . What if we cannot see right off the green fields of Canaan; Moses could not. . . . We must snap the chains of Satan and educate ourselves and our children."[30] The need for education is indeed the argument or one of the arguments of the biblical text, as we will see. The same point is made by a Latin American priest, writing in the 1960s and thinking of the Israelite murmurings: the wilderness period is a time of hardship and struggle, "a gradual pedagogy of successes and failures" in the course of a "long march."[31]

But "gradual pedagogy" is a euphemistic description of the lesson Moses taught the people at the foot of the mountain—a lesson written in blood. The mobilization of the Levites and the killing of the idol worshippers constitute, from the standpoint of politics, an absolutely crucial moment in the transition from house of bondage to promised land. I shall describe it, because this is the way it was described in the early modern period, as the first revolutionary purge. The word "purge" was brought into the vocabulary of revolution by the English Puritans:[32] they took it, I think, from Ezekiel 20, where the prophet recounts the Exodus story and promises the Babylonian exiles a new Exodus and a new wilderness:

> Like as I pleaded with your fathers in the wilderness . . . so will I plead with you, saith the Lord God. And I will cause you to pass under the rod, and I will bring you into the bond of the covenant: And I will purge out from among you . . . them that transgress against me: I will bring them forth out of the country where they sojourn [but] they shall not enter into the land of Israel . . . (20:36–38)

The rabbis tended to talk of the "purgings" of the wilderness period as if they were a kind of law enforcement, but even they saw in the killing of the idol worshippers at the foot of Mount Sinai a political act of a special kind. For them, its extraordinary character was revealed by an omission in the text. "And [Moses] said unto them: thus saith the Lord God of Israel, put every man his sword by his side. . . ." But God's command is not given; God nowhere orders the killing of the idol worshippers. Did Moses invent the command? Was he—once again my reference is deliberately anachronistic—a Machiavellian prince and liberator? This is the Moses that Machiavelli describes in his *Discourses:* "He who reads the Bible with discernment will see that, in order that Moses might set about making laws and institutions, he had to kill a very

59

great number of men. . . ."[33] And isn't it easier to do what in any case must be done if the prince can claim divine authority? Some of the rabbis took the Machiavellian view:

> Moses reasoned with himself and said in his heart: If I say to the Israelites, kill every man his brother, they will answer me: On what grounds do you slay three thousand men in one day? He therefore invoked the honor of the Most High and said: "Thus saith the Lord. . . ."[34]

Other rabbis argued that God had indeed issued the command, but it was too awful to record. Awful, because brothers and neighbors were slain; awful, because the slaughter was summary justice: the idol worshippers were killed without warning and without judgment. Thus the medieval commentator Nachmanides: "This was an emergency measure . . . since there was no proper judicial warning; for who had warned them of the consequences of their crime? . . . It was an order orally imparted to Moses . . . and not recorded."[35] An emergency measure: an act, so to speak, of state.

Whether the command originated with God or with Moses, it was a momentous command. After many of the other murmurings, the people who challenged Moses were killed, but not as the idol worshippers are killed here. In the other cases, the killing is God's own work, further displays of His absolute power and His terrible anger: "and his anger was kindled; and the fire of the Lord burnt among them . . . " (Num. 11:1). Only here are the agents of destruction human: Moses himself and a band of associates who rally round him at the critical moment —and who become later on the Levitical priesthood. Modern biblical scholars typically describe this part of the story as a late addition (assuming now that the whole story isn't a late addition) designed to justify the role of the Levites.[36] But the story as we have it makes a lot of sense, if not always happy sense. The pedagogy of the desert is not only slow, it is uneven; some people or some groups of people learn more quickly than others. Some of them commit themselves more wholeheartedly to the covenant, shape themselves to the new model of the chosen people, internalize the law at a time when for the others the law is still an external command, a threat to their Egyptian habits. Moses' call "Who is on the Lord's side?" draws these new-modeled men to *his* side, divides the community, creates a subgroup—we might call it a vanguard—whose members anticipate, at least in their own minds, the "free people" of the future. In fact, they become the magistrates of the future, the priests and bureaucrats. And meanwhile, in the present, they rule by force; they are the enemies of "graciousness" and gradualism.

→ new tyranny (→ USSR, China)

IV

MOSES' call to the Levites is a political act of the first importance, and as such it has figured significantly in Western political thought. I want now to look at some examples of its citation and use; I don't propose an exercise in the history of ideas, but a further effort to grasp the meaning of the text through a critique of interpretations. Here the text poses a clear question about political violence and the agents of violence, and so it has been read over the years. Or not read: for one can always refuse to engage the question by ignoring Exodus 32. In his

Antiquities of the Jews, Josephus retells the Exodus story in considerable detail but skips the incident of the golden calf, reporting only that "there fell a contention" among the people waiting for the return of Moses.[37] I suspect that Josephus wanted his readers to think that the Zealots of his own time were the first radical enthusiasts in Jewish history and that they had no biblical warrant. In fact, the Levites or the proto-Levites were the first, and they signaled their enthusiasm with the sword.

When can the sword rightly be used? And by whom can it rightly be used? These are central issues in political thought, and for many years whenever they were discussed Exodus 32 figured in the discussions. When Saint Augustine, for example, finally brought himself to defend the persecution of heretical Christians by the Roman state, he justified his new position with an interpretation of the killing of the idol worshippers. The sword looked the same, he admitted, in the hands of Roman magistrates and Donatist heretics, but it served different purposes:

> When good and bad do the same actions and suffer the same afflictions, they are to be distinguished not by what they do or suffer, but by the causes of each: for example, Pharaoh oppressed the people of God by hard bondage; Moses afflicted the same people by severe correction when they were guilty of impiety [Augustine refers here to Exod. 32:27]: their actions were alike; but they were not alike in the motive of regard to the people's welfare—the one inflated by the lust of power, the other inflamed by love.[38]

"Inflamed by love" is a nice reading of the biblical text "and Moses' anger waxed hot." But what is most interesting about this passage, and other of Augustine's references to the story of the golden calf, is the entire absence of the Levites. Augustine wanted to defend the activity of magistrates; he didn't mean to invite private men to do the Lord's work, and so he had nothing to say about Moses' call for volunteers. Like Josephus, he fell silent at a crucial point. During the years of the Crusades, however, private men were loudly called and apparently the call was justified by invocations of Exodus 32. For had not Moses said: "Put *every* man his sword by his side . . . "? This at any rate was the passage that Thomas Aquinas had to deal with when he undertook to answer the Christian radicals of his own time. He answered by stressing the first part of Moses' speech: "Thus saith the Lord God of Israel. . . . " The Levites acted at God's direct command (Moses was nothing more than a messenger), and so the slaughter of the idol worshippers was "properly" His act and not their own.[39] And God doesn't issue such commands, doesn't act in this way, anymore. Years later, Hugo Grotius repeated Aquinas' argument: he attributed the severity of the Levitical punishment to "divine counsel," and he insisted, with a fine show of agnostic trepidation, that such counsel cannot be a guide to contemporary politics: "No conclusive inference can be drawn . . . its depths we cannot sound . . . we are liable to run into error."[40]

For John Calvin and his followers, this sort of thing was mere cowardice. Exodus 32 was obviously a precedent, and it was a precedent that they were more willing than Augustine or Aquinas to set within a history. Since they thought they were reenacting the entire Exodus, they were able to read the entire text. The journey through the wilderness was in part a metaphor for their own politics, and in part a model. They too had escaped from (popish) oppression only to find themselves caught up in a long and difficult struggle with their own people: God's elect against what a Puritan preacher, citing Exodus, called "the opposing rage of a hardened multitude."[41] In Calvin's mind it was more important that the Levites had killed brethren than that they had killed idolators: "You shall show yourselves rightly zealous of God's service," he told his Genevan audience, "in that you kill your own brethren without sparing, so as in this case the order of nature be put under foot, to show that God is above all."[42] The political point was made even more clearly by John Knox in a brief comment on the same text: "God's word draweth his elect after it, against worldly appearance, against natural affections, and against civil statutes and constitutions."[43] As that last phrase suggests, the distinction between magistrates and private men meant nothing to Knox. God Himself gave employment to saints out of office.

But the work was never easy. Even "meek Moses," a Puritan preacher told the House of Commons in 1643, sometimes had to be a "man of blood."[44] The Puritans were not surprised to find the English people, freed from "bondage under the regal power," resisting any further deliverance. For hadn't the Israelites provoked and enraged the God who elected them, as Cromwell said, "through unbelief, murmuring, repining, and other temptations and sins?"[45] Why should the English be different? And God had responded harshly, sometimes with His own hand, sometimes through His appointed agents. It wasn't necessary to read the text with Machiavellian "discernment" to see the harshness; one had only to read it— though perhaps it helped to find oneself (or to imagine oneself) marching over the difficult terrain between bondage and promise. There was no way to reach the promised land except to overcome the opponents of the march and then drive on the reluctant marchers. So it seemed, at any rate: revolutions produce hard men and hard women. One can hear the hardness again and again in the 1640s, often with an Exodus "proof." "The divine policy and heavenly remedy to recover a commonwealth and church endangered," Samuel Faircloth told the Commoners as early as 1641, ". . . is that those that have authority under God do totally abolish and extirpate all the cursed things whereby it was disturbed."[46] The "cursed things" are doubled here: Faircloth's text makes it clear that he includes the idols and the idol worshippers. And those that have authority under God are first of all the Commoners, but soon the purged Commoners, and finally the parliament of saints.

Roughly three centuries later, Lincoln Steffens found in the Exodus story a complete vindication of Leninist politics, that is, of dictatorship and terror. He repeats Augustine's distinction between Moses' and Pharaoh's use of the sword in appropriately modern language: "Whenever a nation is setting up a new system of laws and customs, it has a red terror; whenever it is defending an old system, it has a white terror."[47] Indeed, Leninism seems to be an old story: the slavish people, incapable of liberating themselves, incapable by themselves of imagining what liberation might be like; the revolutionary leader who comes from the outside, whose life experience is entirely different from that of the oppressed men and women he leads; the band of militants, recruited from among the people, but also separated from them to form an organized and disciplined cadre; and finally, the constant purging of the people by the militants. To locate these elements in the Exodus is not to misread the text, to impose Lenin's theory upon it. I would rather say that Lenin's theory of revolution (I shall leave aside his practice) is greatly strengthened by its "fit" with the Exodus text.

Nor are rabbinic readings entirely at variance with the

Leninist reading. Martin Buber is faithful to three thousand years of Jewish interpretation when he writes in his *Moses* that the Exodus was "the kind of liberation which cannot be brought about by anyone who grew up as a slave."[48] Moses is separate from the people in his growing up, and later on he separates himself again. Immediately after the incident of the golden calf, "Moses took the tabernacle and pitched it without the camp, afar off from the camp" (Exod. 33:7). The standard rabbinic explanation—no reason is given in the text itself—is that Moses moved the tabernacle because of "the people's sin with the calf."[49] Neither God nor His deputy could dwell any longer in their midst. One might say, more sadly, that neither God nor Moses could dwell among a people whose brothers, companions, and neighbors they (one or the other of them anyway) had ordered killed. So the idol, even after it has been destroyed, casts its shadow over the camp, and the people are led not, as one would expect a covenanted people to be led, from their midst and by one of their own, but from the outside, by an outsider.

V

BUT the story can be told differently. If there is a Leninist reading, there is also, as I have already suggested, a social-democratic reading—which stresses the indirection of the march and the role of Moses as the pedagogue of the people and their defender before God (and which de-emphasizes the story of the golden calf). Moses is capable of anger, but he is also the embodiment of kindness: a "man of blood" but also "meek Moses." "And Moses was very meek, above all the men which were upon the face of the earth" (Num. 12:3). In one of the rebellions against his authority, the tribal leaders Dathan and Abiram accuse Moses of trying to make himself "altogether a prince over us" (Num. 16:13). But Moses doesn't in fact rule like a prince; he is portrayed again and again arguing with the people, much as he argues with God; in neither case does he always get his way. He is rather more successful with God than with the people, and it is worth noting that the forty years in the wilderness are his achievement. When the Israelites reach the Negev, the desert south of Canaan, they send spies into the promised land, and the spies bring back a frightening report: the inhabitants are as large and as powerful as giants, "and we were in our own sight as grasshoppers, and so were we in their sight" (Num. 13:-33). And then the people once again murmur against Moses and want to "make a captain and . . . return to Egypt" (14:4). They were as "sore afraid" in the desert as they were at the sea, Egyptian slaves still, though they had put many miles between themselves and their former masters. God is furious, as usual, and ready once again to destroy the people, but Moses intercedes and He settles for the forty years. The term is chosen for a purpose: so that all those Israelites who were twenty years old or older at the time of the "going out" from Egypt will die natural deaths in the wilderness (three score years, rather than three score and ten, is taken here as the conventional span of life, though Moses himself is granted a double span). Lincoln Steffens takes this to be the chief political lesson of the Exodus: "The grown-ups must die." And so he interprets the text to mean that "the Lord God killed off the whole of the Egyptian generation of the Jews."[50] But in Numbers 14, as in other accounts of Israelite murmurings, only some of the people are killed. The greater number of the slaves live out their lives and raise a new generation of freeborn children.

Moses teaches this new generation the laws and rituals of Israel's new religion. He accepts Jethro's advice, leaves the daily government to others, and takes for himself another task: "And thou shalt teach them ordinances and laws, and shalt show them the way wherein they must walk and the work that they must do" (Exod. 18:20). This is how Moses is remembered in the Jewish interpretive tradition—not as a prince or a judge or even a "founder" (though in first-century Alexandria Philo describes him as "the best of all lawgivers in all countries, better in fact than any that have ever arisen among either the Greeks or the barbarians," and Machiavelli and Rousseau arrive at a roughly similar estimate).[51] For the Jews generally he is a prophet and teacher, *Moshe rabenu*, Moses our rabbi.[52] He is a successful teacher, which must mean that he finds apt pupils; and he makes his pupils teachers in their turn: "And these words which I command thee this day shall be in thine heart: And thou shalt teach them diligently unto thy children . . . " (Deut. 6:6–7). The result is that the Israelites at the Jordan are very different from the Israelites at the sea: they are ready at last to fight their own battles. In one of his last speeches, Moses is able to say:

> When thou goest out to battle against thine enemies, and seest horses, and chariots, and a people more than thou [the phrases recall Pharaoh's army at the sea], be not afraid of them: for the Lord thy God is with thee, which brought thee up out of the land of Egypt.   (Deut. 20:1)

And he can feel some confidence that the people will not in fact be afraid. They are no longer "as grasshoppers" in their own eyes. They are a "political society," committed to one another and to the covenant that binds them together. This is the achievement of the four decades in the wilderness.

Was it the purging or the teaching that made the decisive difference? The text can be read either way; that is why it has been read so long and so often. Over the years, it has more frequently been used by those who want to imitate the Levites at Mount Sinai and coerce and kill their enemies in the revolutionary camp. Such people have greater need of religious or historical justification. And at some point, I suppose, the counterrevolution must be defeated if Egyptian bondage is ever to be left behind. It is important to stress, however, what the text makes clear, that the counterrevolution has deep roots; it cannot be defeated by force alone. Indeed, God and the Levites could easily kill all the people who yearn for the fleshpots (or the idols) of Egypt. But then the Levites would arrive in the promised land virtually alone, and that would not be a fulfillment of the promise. The promise is for the people, and the people can only move in gradual stages from bondage to freedom.

In the text as we have it, the portrayal of the people is consistently harsh. But they are not consistently described as slavish and servile; they are also described as "stiff-necked" (by God Himself at the time of the golden calf episode) and stubborn. So they are not wholly dispirited. And to be stubborn, even in the face of God, is not wholly unattractive. Sometimes the people seem less like a slavish rabble than like ordinary men and women recalcitrant in the face of God's demand that they be something more than ordinary. For it is not God's purpose merely to bring them to the promised land. The promise itself is more complicated than milk and honey—as I will try to show in chapter 4—and the resistance of the people has a certain saving quality, best illustrated by a midrashic story. When the Israelites were finally allowed to leave the holy mountain, it is said, they rose early, folded their tents, packed their belongings, and marched as fast as they could—not for one day, as they were commanded, but for three days. They didn't want any more laws.[53] It is a nice story; we recognize ourselves in it, even though we have never lived, or think we have never lived, in Egypt. I would add just one word: when they marched away from the mountain, they marched toward the promised land, not "back for Egypt." They had their own vision of a better life, and sometimes they had the courage of their vision. That is why they were able, as Rabbi Eliezer said, to march into the wilderness in the first place; and this is why they were able to commit themselves to the covenant at Sinai. The Hegelian and the Leninist views of the Exodus have no place for the covenant, but it is central to the Jewish tradition and to much later revolutionary thought. And if the Israelites were too stiff-necked to live up to all of its requirements, they were also too stiff-necked ever to forget it entirely.

THREE

The Covenant:

A Free People

I

THE GREAT paradox of the Exodus, and of all subsequent liberation struggles, is the people's simultaneous willingness and unwillingness to put Egypt behind them. They yearn to be free, and they yearn to escape their new freedom. They want laws but not too many; they both accept and resist the discipline of the march. The biblical narrative tells this paradoxical story with a frankness not often repeated in the literature of liberation. Thus far I have stressed one side of the paradox, the resistance, the murmurings against God and Moses, which begin in Egypt itself and are continuous, or at least recurrent, through the desert years. Popular resistance has its source, so we are told, in the slavishness of the Israelites; it has another source in their stiff-necked spiritedness. The Exodus, after all, would look very different had the people simply transferred their slavish obedience from Pharaoh to God. But God's service is radically unlike pharaonic slavery (even though the two are named by the same

Hebrew word). The difference is this: slavery is begun and sustained by coercion, while service is begun and sustained by covenant.

Covenant is the political invention of the Book of Exodus. Modern scholars have explored in detail the structural and verbal similarities between the Sinai covenant and the ancient "suzerainty treaty" in which a vassal ruler acknowledges the supremacy of a high king.[1] The explorations are both exciting and illuminating, for they place the Exodus in its time. But they extend to structure and vocabulary only; they tell us little about the agents of the covenant or its subject matter. There is no precedent for a treaty between God and an entire people or for a treaty whose conditions are literally the laws of morality. Focusing on the covenant, I shall be able to explain why popular recalcitrance and vanguard initiative, murmuring and purging, make only part of the Exodus story. Indeed, it is central to the narrative strategy of the author (or the final editor) of the story that the purges come after the covenant, though the murmurings begin before. The ultimate justification for the purges, if they are justified at all, lies not in divine will but in popular willingness.

There is a tradition, hinted at by the prophet Ezekiel (20:8), that God's punishments actually began in Egypt along with the first murmurings.[2] But this tradition has no place in the biblical narrative. It would make God look too much like Pharaoh. Moses, to be sure, seeks the consent of the Israelites to their own liberation (Exod. 4:29–31), but the consent of slaves is not morally binding, and when the people, frightened and dispirited, renege, God does not hold them responsible. They are not punished for their complaints in Egypt nor for their desire to turn back at the sea nor even for the first rebellions in the wilderness: for they have not yet committed themselves to God and His commandments. The covenant waits until they have savored their freedom—and marched as far as the holy mountain. There they stand between Egypt and the promised land, and they have to choose. Spinoza suggests that they are, at this moment of freedom, in a state of nature.[3] Natural liberty is the immediate consequence of deliverance—not for the Israelites alone, presumably, but for any newly liberated people. And then, since natural liberty is in practice unendurable, the covenant—one or another covenant anyway—necessarily follows. Given the tribal organization of the Israelites and the ongoing authority of their elders, this is not a sociologically plausible account, but it does make moral sense. For it isn't the elders but the people themselves who accept the covenant. "And all the people answered together, and said, All that the Lord hath spoken we will do" (Exod. 19:8). The old hierarchies are suspended; the covenant is a solemn commitment entered into by free men.

And women too: according to the Midrash, God at Sinai remembered the mistake He had made in delivering His original command about the tree of knowledge to Adam alone and not to Eve with him. "If I do not now call unto the women *first*, they will nullify the Torah."[4] Indeed, the Sinai covenant is radically inclusive. Exodus 19 reads simply "all the people answered . . . " but Deuteronomy 29 elaborates:

Ye stand this day all of you before the Lord your God; your captains of your tribes, your elders, and your officers, with all the men of Israel, your little ones, your wives, and thy stranger that is in thy camp, from the hewer of thy wood unto the drawer of thy water: That thou shouldest enter into a covenant with the Lord thy God . . . That he may establish thee today for a people unto himself . . . (29:10–13)

The covenant is a founding act, creating alongside the old association of tribes a new nation composed of willing members. In Egypt, the Israelites are a "people" insofar as they share tribal memories—or, more importantly, insofar as they share the experience of oppression. (It is Pharaoh who first uses the word "people" to describe them.) Their identity, like that of all men and women before liberation, is something that has happened to them. Only with the covenant do they make themselves into a people in the strong sense, capable of sustaining a moral and political history, capable of obedience and also of stiff-necked resistance, of marching forward and of sliding back. Hence the centrality of the covenant and the importance of reflecting upon its precise character.

In the traditional tales and folk elaborations that cluster around the Exodus, the covenant is often described as if it were a kind of bargain and God a kind of salesman, hawking His commandments around the world, coming to the Israelites only after He has been rejected elsewhere.[5] If Israel, in one version of the story, is quick to accept the commandments, in another version the people have to be persuaded—and not by promises alone. Why, asks an early Midrash, didn't God begin the Torah by proclaiming His law? The answer is given in a political parable. This may be compared, it is said, to a

king who entered a province and said to the people: May I be your king? But the people said to him: Have you done anything good for us that you should rule over us? What did he do then? He built a city wall for them, he brought

76

in the water supply for them, and he fought their battles.
Then when he said to them: May I be your king? they said
to him: Yes, yes. Likewise God. He brought the Israelites
out of Egypt, divided the sea for them, sent down the
manna for them . . . [and] He fought for them the battle
with Amalek. Then He said to them: I am to be your king.
And they said to Him: Yes, yes.[6]

The author can't quite bring himself to put a question into
God's mouth, as he had done with the king. But his account captures the form of the ancient treaties, which
always begin with a list of benefits conferred, and the
spirit of the preamble to the commandments: "I am the
Lord thy God, which . . . brought thee out of the land of
Egypt, out of the house of bondage" (Exod. 20:2). The
same emphasis on God's record of benefits can be found
in a sermon preached to the House of Commons in 1642,
urging a new covenant.

Israel's experience is on record in Holy Writ for our encouragement. We may add God's dispensations in this
kingdom. Who in the year Eighty-eight sunk and scattered
the Spanish navy called invincible? Who broke the neck
of the Popish powder plot? . . . And who lately composed
the dangerous differences betwixt England and Scotland?[7]

These accounts miss, however, the real conditionality of
the covenant, which has less to do with the past performances of God than with the future performances of the
people.

It is useful to distinguish the Sinai covenant and its later
repetitions from the covenants with Noah and Abraham
(and then from the covenant with David, modeled on
these latter two).[8] The earlier covenants have the form of
absolute and unconditional promises delivered by God.
Thus the promises to Abraham: "I will make thee exceed-

ing fruitful. . . . And I will give unto thee, and to thy seed after thee, the land wherein thou art a stranger, all the land of Canaan . . ." (Gen. 17:6,8). At Sinai, by contrast, God's promises are radically contingent: "If ye will obey my voice indeed, and keep my covenant, then ye shall be a peculiar treasure unto me . . . " (Exod. 19:5). The absolute promises play into both royalist and messianic thought. They are comforting but not energizing; they invite political action only from the deputies of God—which is what kings and self-proclaimed messiahs take themselves to be. The role of Moses as divine messenger is also rooted in the Abrahamic covenant; before God summons Moses at the burning bush, He remembers "his covenant with Abraham, with Isaac, and with Jacob" (Exod. 2:24). The deliverance from Egypt is unconditional; it doesn't depend on the moral conduct of the slaves. But it is crucial to the Exodus story that this deliverance brings Israel only into the wilderness, only to Sinai, where the conditions of any further advance are revealed. "Moreover," as Saadya Gaon writes, "our teacher Moses felt that it was not sufficient to state the positive case by saying, 'If ye shall keep,' or 'If thou shalt hearken,' and then to leave it to the people to put the opposite to themselves, but he pointed out to them that in case they did not fulfill the conditions, God would not fulfill [the] promises. In inverting the terms, he made it clear that . . . 'If thou shalt forget the Lord thy God . . . as the nations that the Lord maketh to perish before you, so shall ye perish' (Deut. 8:19–20). . . . " By contrast, Saadya continues, "God has attached no conditions to [the messianic promises], much less inverted the terms."[9] The messianic deliverance will bypass both the wilderness and the mountain.

This distinction plays a part in later revolutionary history. Among the English Puritans, for example, it is possible to make out two groups of ministers, the one committed to what I want to call Exodus politics, expounding the Sinai covenant, the other committed to (or at least experimenting with) apocalyptic and millennialist politics, expounding the Abrahamic covenant. "In the one," writes John Wilson in a study of political sermons during the 1640s, "human agency was invited to respond to divine purposes; in the other, the independence of the divine initiative from human agency was celebrated."[10] The political character of liberation theology in Latin America today is determined by a similar contrast. Here the stress is on the practical invitation of Exodus politics, while millennialist celebration, despite the Christian convictions of the liberation theologians, is relatively neglected. I shall have more to say about these alternatives in the next chapter and again in the conclusion. I am interested now in the nature of the human agency upon which the response to divine purposes depends.

Whose covenant is it? When the Levites gather around Moses at the foot of the mountain, they claim, in effect, that the covenant is theirs. And indeed, the call for volunteers—"Who is on the Lord's side? let him come unto me"—is a common feature of covenantal politics. Exodus 32 is consciously echoed by the priest Mattathias at the beginning of the Maccabean revolt: "All who are zealous for the . . . Torah, who uphold the covenant, march out after me!" (1 Macc. 2:27). But the Levites are only the enforcers of the covenant and the Maccabees only its defenders. The covenant itself rests on a broader base, else it could never legitimately be enforced or defended. At Sinai, the entire people committed itself, not through representatives or proxies but each individual in his own voice. When the covenant is reiterated at Shechem, the text suggests that it is heads of families, not individuals, who join together. Joshua says to the people: "And if it seem evil unto you to serve the Lord, choose you this day whom ye will serve . . . but as for me and my house, we will serve the Lord" (Josh. 24:15). In the commentaries on Exodus 19 and 24, however, the rabbis are surprisingly insistent on the individualistic character of the covenant and on the explicitness of popular consent. The covenant reflected what we might usefully call the general will of the Israelites, but this was a general will built, in good Rousseauian fashion, out of the wills of independent, noncommunicating individuals.

> *And all the people answered together* (Exod. 19:8). They did not give this answer with hypocrisy, nor did they get it one from the other, but all of them made up their minds alike and said: "All that the Lord hath spoken we will do."[11]

It is clear, moreover, that the people understood the requirements of the covenant; their consent was not openended: "All that the Lord *hath spoken. . . . "* Again, the rabbis emphasize the point. Before the covenant was made, one of them writes, "Moses read aloud to the people all of the Torah [not just the Ten Commandments but the whole of the Five Books], that they might know exactly what they were taking upon themselves."[12]

The people could have chosen differently, though God would presumably have been astonished had they done so. The covenant introduces into the Exodus story a radical voluntarism that sits uneasily with the account of the original deliverance—where God, absolute and almighty, makes all the decisions and the people, as Hegel wrote, do nothing for themselves. Hegel fails to mention the events at Sinai, where it is the people who decide. But this combination of divine willfulness and popular choice, providence and covenant, determinism and freedom is characteristic of Exodus politics and of all later versions of radical and revolutionary politics too. We can see it most clearly among the Puritans, whose covenant theology, modeled on the Exodus, is hardly consistent with the theology of predestination: and yet, the two coexisted over a long period of time.[13] The idea of divine election (or historical inevitability) provides, perhaps, a necessary background for radical politics. Who would take the required risks, who would march into the wilderness or challenge the "giants" of Canaan, without some sense of an assured future? At the same time, the experience of making choices and accepting risks generates the very different ideas of commitment and consent. At Sinai, in any case, the people decide, and that implies that they have what they seemed to lack in Egypt, the capacity for decision. They are possessed not only of natural liberty but also of free will.

"Everything lies in the hands of God," according to an often repeated talmudic maxim, "except the fear of God."[14] The moral life of humanity, and therefore its political life too, is entirely in human hands. And at the moment when they actually take their life into their hands, the people are not craven and despondent but courageous. Standing at Sinai, they embody the excellence of man. Thus Saadya, citing the Deuteronomic account of the covenant: "God . . . gave man the ability to obey Him, placing it as it were in his hands, endowed him with power and free will, and commanded him to choose that which is good. . . . "[15] Power and free will are gifts of God, different from the more particular gift of deliverance, making it possible for man to cooperate, if not in the deliverance itself, then in the long-term work required to make deliverance permanent. Saadya would have said, of course, that man is free only when he does cooperate: to return to Egypt is to enslave oneself. Here again is the doctrine of positive freedom, which is in no sense an invention of Rousseau's *Social Contract* but an enduring feature of covenant theology. The transition from its theological to its political version is nicely illustrated in a speech by John Winthrop (the American Moses, according to Cotton Mather) in 1645. Winthrop is attacking opponents who must have appeared to him as New World murmurers, and in the course of his attack he announces a theory of freedom and obligation:

> The other kind of liberty I call civil or federal, it may also be termed moral, in reference to the covenant between God and man, in the moral laws, and the politic covenants and constitutions amongst men themselves. This liberty is the proper end and object of authority, and cannot subsist without it; and it is a liberty to that only which is good, just, and honest.[16]

We may wonder at that last sentence. But perhaps all it means is that those men and women who, faced with the Deuteronomic choice, "I have set before you life and death" (30:19), choose death, will not escape retribution (will not escape what they have chosen). The retribution makes sense because they have chosen freely, and so there is in fact a liberty to that which is evil, though not a lasting liberty: one doesn't get off scot-free. But the important thing here, in the Exodus story and in Saadya's philosophical commentary and in Winthrop's political enactment, is the conviction that the people are capable, by themselves, of choosing life and then of living up to the moral law. They can promise and keep their promises. In fact, of course, the Israelites don't keep their promises, or many of them don't; the later history of Israel is a tale of "doing evil" and then of divine punishment. What legitimates the punishment and makes it comprehensible, however, is the shared assumption that the people are capable of doing good. <u>The human agents of the covenant</u> <u>are, in contemporary philosophical language,</u> *moral agents.*

II

THE COVENANT itself is only briefly described in the Book of Exodus; a great deal of room is left for the theological, and then the political, imagination. But the text also imposes certain problems. And so it is no accident that rabbinic commentary anticipates, in its own idiom, the central issues of the early modern <u>theory of consent.</u> For the social and governmental contracts of the sixteenth and seventeenth centuries have their origin in the Exodus literature, where the idea is first put forward that obligation and allegiance are rooted, and can only rightly be rooted, in the agreement of individual men and women. One can also argue for the influence of the feudal oath and the complex system of vassalage on later contract theory; many historians have done so.[17] But the stronger line, the line most often drawn in the tracts and pamphlets of radical publicists, runs from the <u>covenant to the contract.</u> This is not to say that seventeenth-century revolutionaries knew the rabbinic interpretations—a few of them probably did— only that the same biblical texts generated similar religious and political ideas. Consider, for example, the debate among the rabbis about the number of covenants made at Sinai. One rabbi said that 603,550 covenants were made, each adult male (<u>the women are left out here</u>) pledging himself to God. But another claimed that every one of these 603,550 covenants was made 603,550 times: the men pledged themselves not only to God but also to one another. "What is the issue between them? Rabbi Mesharsheya said, The issue between them is that of personal responsibility and responsibility for others."[18] Is the individual bound only to observe the laws himself or is he bound to see to it that they are collectively observed? Is he bound to act justly or to make sure that justice is done? The second view has the more radical implications, and it is the second view that wins out in secular political thought. The victorious formulation combines the two rabbinic claims, substituting the people as a whole for God. Thus the preamble to the Massachusetts constitution of 1780: "The body politic is formed by a voluntary association of individuals: it is a social compact, by which the whole people covenants with each citizen, and each citizen with the whole people. . . ."[19] Each citizen, then, has a right and perhaps a duty to concern himself with what "the whole people" do.

It follows from a covenant of this sort that the individuals who commit themselves are moral equals. "There is," in the words of a modern biblical scholar, "a fundamental equality of status so far as Yahweh is concerned, or to put things right way round, an equality of responsibility."[20] The social consequences of covenantal equality I shall leave for the next chapter, where I consider the meaning of "a kingdom of priests and a holy nation." Here I want only to describe the way in which covenanted individuals, and not the caste of priests, come to replace Moses as the teachers of the law, how they take on responsibility for the continuity of the covenant. Continuity is a central issue in consent theory, and it is a central issue, too, in the Exodus literature, beginning with the Deuteronomic account of the covenant, the first commentary. Moses' success lies in the fact that he finds successors not among the few but among the many. The same competence that makes it possible for individuals to join in the covenant in the first place also makes it possible for them to introduce their children to the covenant. What they do is to "remember" the Exodus story.

> And when thy son asketh thee in time to come, saying, What mean the testimonies [Hebrew *'edoth*, literally "pacts," an alternative term for the covenant], and the statutes, and the judgments, which the Lord our God hath commanded you? Then thou shalt say unto thy son, We were Pharaoh's bondsmen in Egypt; and the Lord brought us out of Egypt with a mighty hand..." (Deut. 6:20–21).

There is a philosophical difficulty here, which is expressed by the pronouns. The son asks about the laws that God "hath commanded *you*," excluding himself from the obligation to obey. The father replies, "*We* were Pharaoh's bondsmen, . . ." including his son in the covenantal history. How in fact is consent passed on from father to son? How is the radical voluntarism of the revolutionary period sustained? Not merely by expounding the Exodus to one's children but by encouraging them imaginatively to relive the moment of deliverance. The encouragement is explicit in the Haggadah: "In every generation let each man look upon himself as if *he* came forth out of Egypt."[21] Moses' argument in Deuteronomy is more straightforward, avoiding the "as if" formulation: "The Lord made not this covenant with our fathers, but with us, even us, who are all of us here alive this day" (5:3). And again, in a passage that has been much commented on: "Neither with you only do I make this covenant. . . . But with him that standeth here with us this day . . . and also with him that is not here with us this day" (29:14–15). But this assumes that the imaginative reliving of the Exodus experience will always work, producing in each successive generation a new commitment. What if it doesn't work? Moses pursues the difficulty in his last Deuteronomic sermon. What if there should appear among the people a "man, or woman, or family, or tribe, whose heart turneth away . . . from the Lord our God?" The answer is plain enough: "The Lord will not spare him . . . the anger of the Lord and His jealousy shall smoke against that man . . ." (29:18,20). In Spain, in the years before the Expulsion, when many Jews "turned away" from the covenant, these passages from Deuteronomy were hotly debated, and the obvious question was asked: "Who gave the generation of the wilderness which stood at the foot of Mount Sinai the power of obligating all those who would arise after them? . . . This is surely not a legitimate obligation."[22]

The Spanish-Jewish philosopher Don Isaac Abravanel answers this question with an argument that comes very close to the later theory of tacit consent. The service of God is a permanent commitment, Abravanel insists, because the Jews permanently enjoy the fruits of that service, freedom from Egyptian oppression, the moral law, and the promised land.[23] This is an odd argument to make to a people living in exile from the land and cruelly persecuted. I suppose that Abravanel believed, and perhaps he was right to believe, that the familial and communal life of the Jews preserved somehow the three divine gifts —and the experience of that life sustained the covenantal commitment. "Our exile cannot be compared to the Egyptian bondage," writes a commentator on the Haggadah. "The deliverance from Pharaoh's servitude was final, and we attained . . . an everlasting freedom, sealed by the giving of the Torah."[24] Participation in what a modern

scholar calls the decentralized religious democracy of Israel, where every adult (or at least every adult male) interprets the Torah in his own family, constitutes an implicit
renewal of the covenant.[25] But it is still unclear why God
has any moral reason, since jealousy by itself is not a
moral reason, for punishing a "wicked son," say, who
drops out of the life of the family. Tacit consent works
only for men and women who really do delight in the
divine gifts, who know with certainty that they have been
delivered.

But perhaps we should read the Deuteronomic passages
as an argument for hypothetical rather than tacit consent.
The father invites the son to ask what he himself would
have done had he stood at the foot of Sinai and then to
live in the light of his answer. He must also, of course,
imagine himself newly freed from Egyptian bondage, fed
with manna, experiencing the theophany. And then how
can he, who is not only free but rational and morally
competent, pretend that he would have said no? I am
inclined to prefer an argument that depends on the vivid-
ness of the present rather than the past, but this is not an
implausible version of the Deuteronomic text (or of the
Passover Haggadah). And on the most crucial point, this
version agrees with the earlier one: however the problem
of continuity is resolved, it must be resolved for free and
equal individuals, who hold the covenant, and the covenantal texts, in their own hands. When Moses carries the
tablets down from the mountain (for the second time), he
hands them over to the people, not, it is worth repeating,
to the caste of priests. This is the meaning of the passage
that I quoted at the end of the last chapter:

> And these words, which I command thee this day, shall be
> in thine heart: And thou shalt teach them diligently unto

thy children, and shalt talk of them when thou sittest in
thine house, and when thou walkest by the way, and when
thou liest down, and when thou riseth up.   (Deut. 6:6–7)

Perhaps we should say simply that the covenant is carried
forward on a flood of talk: argument and analysis, folkloric expansion, interpretation and reinterpretation.

But the covenant is also periodically and collectively
renewed. The radical voluntarism of the biblical account
can't be contained by the doctrines of tacit and hypothetical consent. At moments of crisis, the people must meet
and reaffirm their commitment. These reaffirmations
don't have a merely ritual character, as if their purpose
were to regain the magical efficacy of the original covenanting. They are moral acts; their purpose is to sustain
personal and collective obligation (there is no magical
efficacy). I have already referred to the covenant at Shechem, which marks the definitive arrival of Israel in the
promised land. Some four hundred years later, the religious reformation of King Josiah, for which Deuteronomy
itself is the programmatic manifesto, begins with another
public and explicit commitment. "All the people, both
great and small" assembled in Jerusalem, and the young
king "read in their ears all the words of the book of the
covenant . . . And all the people stood to the covenant"
(2 Kings 23:2–3). And again, at the time of the refounding
of the Jewish commonwealth after the Babylonian exile:
for seven days, Ezra the scribe, together with various
priests and Levites, read and expounded the law "before
the men and the women and those that could understand,
and the ears of all the people were attentive unto the book
of the law." And on the eighth day, there was a "solemn
assembly," and a historical sermon focusing mostly on the

Exodus, and then the writing and sealing of a "sure covenant" (Neh. 8:3,18; 9:38).

These covenants don't make for simple continuity, but for interruptions and new beginnings—after backsliding, reform; after exile, return. Here the events of Sinai are reenacted not in fancy but in fact. Similar reenactments have played an important part in Protestant and then in secular politics. The first Protestant example is a literal reiteration of the Sinai covenant. In Geneva in 1537, the triumph of Calvin and his followers was marked by a civic ceremony in which the citizens swore to obey the Ten Commandments, along with the laws of the city. Calvin may not have recognized the importance of popular willingness; as described by a modern historian, the proceedings sound something less than joyful: "groups of people, summoned by the police, gave their adherence."[26] Still, the aim here is similar to that of the biblical writers. Calvin sought to turn the city into a covenanted community, to replace custom, habit, every sort of easy aquiescence in established ways, with explicit (if not necessarily eager) agreement.

This is indeed what reformers and revolutionaries have to do, and the Geneva covenant is soon repeated—though with decreasing biblical literalness—in the Mayflower Compact, in the Scottish National Covenant, in the Solemn League and Covenant of 1643, in the Puritan army's Agreement of the People, in the American constitutions of the 1780s. All these are genuine covenants, depending for their force on the consent of a free (newly free!) people, and all of them look back, more or less distantly, to that moment at Sinai when the Israelites said yes, yes. I don't quite share the view of one of the liberation theologians of Latin America, who writes that the Exodus "has meaning for me only if I am involved in a *present-day* process of liberation."[27] Certainly, the story takes on new meaning to people so involved (or, they gain new insight into what it might originally have meant). But Sinai is a model for popular involvement because of the tradition of vicarious experience that I have been describing. The study of the Bible leads to a view of political action as a kind of communal performance: what happened in Egypt and at Sinai provides a precedent for early modern (and *present-day*) efforts to mobilize men and women for a politics without precedent in their own experience.

III

THE COVENANT makes for responsibility; it is therefore a reason for political action. In Jewish thought, the crucial responsibility that individuals take upon themselves is to live in accordance with divine law. They are pledged to obey God—but also, at least on one interpretation of the covenant, to see to it that God is obeyed. This latter responsibility helps to explain both the role of the biblical prophets and the acceptance of that role by the people (even, though doubtless more reluctantly, by the Israelite and Judean kings). After the incident of the golden calf, revolutionary commitment is gradually institutionalized in the Aaronite and Levitical priesthoods. The priests don't only perform the necessary religious ceremonies, offer the sacrifices, recite the prayers, and so on. They also live a life of ritual purity; they sustain a degree of holiness appropriate to a "holy nation" but not now available to the mass of Israelites. The prophets too substitute themselves for the mass of Israelites—Moses hoped, as we will see, for universal prophecy—but they do so in a different way. Whereas the priests act for the people, the prophets call upon the people to act; and whereas the priests represent the ritual requirements of the covenant, the prophets, denying the centrality of ritual, represent the ethical requirements. The priesthood is the vanguard grown old, the vanguard entrenched, privileged, conservative (this is not to say that individuals can't sometimes recapture the original radicalism of the Levites: Mattathias was a priest of Modi'in). The prophets sustain the pedagogical role of Moses, though their teaching often takes the form of a savage indictment. They stand alongside ordinary men and women who teach the law to their families: the prophets teach the law to the nation. Their indictment reaches from kings and priests to artisans and farmers; they defend the idea of collective responsibility.

[To be a moral agent is not to act rightly but to be capable of acting rightly.] The Israelites are capable, but they often fall short of the demands of the law. And then the prophets come forward to remind them of their commitments. It is a mistake to think of the prophets primarily as religious innovators; nor are they most usefully described as ecstatics or visionaries (though they sometimes had visions) who shatter the mold of Israelite religion. They are religious reformers, and they cast their arguments in a style appropriate to the linearity of Exodus politics: they look back to the deliverance and the covenant and forward to the promises. Gustavo Gutierrez captures the character of their religious (and political) message when he writes that "the prophets . . . heirs to the Mosaic ideal, referred to the past. . . . There they sought inspiration for the construction of a just society. To accept poverty and injustice is to fall back into the . . . servitude which existed before the liberation from Egypt."[28] We can see clearly what prophecy is about in one of the characteristic genres of prophetic argument—the divine lawsuit. Here is an example from Micah (6:2–8):

> Hear ye, O mountains, the Lord's controversy, and ye strong foundations of the earth: for the Lord hath a controversy with his people, and He will plead with Israel. O my people what have I done unto thee? and wherein have I wearied thee? testify against me. For I brought thee up out of the land of Egypt and redeemed thee out of the house of bondage. . . . Will the Lord be pleased with thousands of rams, or with ten thousands of rivers of oil? Shall I give my firstborn for my transgression, the fruit of my body for the sin of my soul? He hath showed thee, O man, what is good; and what doth the Lord require of thee, but to do justly, and to love mercy [the Hebrew is *hesed*, better translated as "convenantal faithfulness and kindness"], and to walk humbly with thy God?

Though the covenant is not explicitly mentioned here, God's controversy with Israel depends upon it, and the history and imagery invoke it.[29] The lawsuit requires the law and the popular commitment to obey the law. And the substance of the law is ethical, not ceremonial: "For I desired mercy [*hesed* again], and not sacrifice; and the knowledge of God more than burnt offerings" (Hos. 6:6).

The divine lawsuit is directed against the people as a whole. Though some of the people are sinners and some, presumably, are not, some are oppressors and some are oppressed, the prophets don't try to rally the faithful or to organize a party. They don't call for volunteers, like Moses at the mountain, to enforce the covenant. In their theology, God is the great enforcer, and He uses external agents—the Assyrians, the Babylonians—to scourge His people. But the call for volunteers is part of the story, and it figures importantly in the Protestant revival of Exodus politics. The divine lawsuit figures, too, though it is sometimes stood on its head. "The covenant giveth to the believer," wrote the Calvinist Samuel Rutherford in his *Lex, Rex* (1644), "a sort of action of law . . . to plead with God in respect of his fidelity. . . . " I am not quite sure of the reference of that last pronoun, but Rutherford's meaning is clear: faithful covenanters are entitled to the promised gifts of a faithful God. What is involved here, however, is only "a sort of action of law," a metaphorical application of covenant theology. Rutherford is aiming, beyond this, at a practical application: "And far more a covenant giveth ground of a civil action and claim to a people . . . against a king. . . . "[30]

The theological argument for this "action and claim" was first worked out by the author of the *Vindiciae Contra Tyrannos* some seventy years before Rutherford wrote, during the French religious wars. In the *Vindiciae*, a systematic effort is made to bring together the Exodus covenant with the later royal covenants described in the Second Book of Kings. God's covenant with David (2 Sam. 7:1–17) is ignored; this has the form of a unilateral divine promise, modeled on the promise to Abraham and constituting, as I have suggested, a centerpiece of royalist ideology. But later kings, particularly in the northern kingdom, sought (or perhaps needed) a different kind of covenantal legitimacy: "And Jehoiada [the high priest] made a covenant between the Lord and the king and the people, that they should be the Lord's people; between the king also and the people" (2 Kings 11:17). This seems simply to bring the king into the Sinai covenant, and so it is interpreted in the *Vindiciae*. So far as the people's obligations are concerned, the later covenant, which includes the king, is identical with the earlier one, in which kings are unknown. "There is the same covenant, the same conditions, the same punishments."[31] From these similarities, the author argues, very much as Jewish commentators had done, for the moral competence of the people—and then moves on to make a new political argument (but one entirely consistent with covenant theology).

> It is a thing most certain, that God hath not [covenanted] in vain, and if the people had not authority to promise and to keep promise, it were vainly lost time to contract or covenant with them. . . . [Hence] all the people . . . do jointly and voluntarily assume, promise and oblige themselves . . . and if either [king or people] be negligent of their covenant, God may justly demand the whole of which of the two he pleaseth, and the more probably of the people . . . for that many cannot slip away so easily as one.[32]

The obligation to oppose idolatrous or wicked kings follows from the claim that men and women who fail in opposition will be called to account by God Himself. The argument is rather like that of soldiers in our own time who refuse to obey military orders, pleading that obedience will open them to criminal charges under international law. So subjects who allow the king "to draw them after strange gods" are liable to punishment by the one God to whom they are committed. (It's the commitment that makes the other gods "strange." They are in any case false, but it is a mistake and not a crime to worship false gods.) The covenant between king and people, depending on its terms, might justify opposition—just as the character of this or that military command might justify disobedience. But it is the covenant with God that provides, at least for believers, a powerful and overriding motive.

Having provided this motive, however, the author of

the *Vindiciae* is unwilling to endorse the action it motivates. Only the lesser magistrates, he insists, can oppose an idolatrous and wicked king—a social qualification on a covenantal argument. Ordinary men and women are included in the covenant only as subjects and vassals, spoken for by their feudal lords. But it is a crucial feature of covenantal argument that each person speaks for himself. Moses is a mediator only in a physical, not in a moral or spiritual, sense, and at the moment of agreement, there is no social or ecclesiastical hierarchy. Responsibility belongs equally to all. By pleading that they must wait for the magistrate, wrote the early Puritan radical and Marian exile, Christopher Goodman, ordinary men and women "slip their heads out of the collar." But the collar is the covenant, God's service, not Pharaoh's, and it is unslippable. Ultimately it must carry the people into the hitherto closed realm of political action. "And though it appears at first sight a great disorder," wrote Goodman, "that the people should take unto them the punishment of transgression, yet when the magistrates . . . cease to do their duty . . . then God giveth the sword into the people's hand and he himself is become immediately their head. . . ."[33]

But this brings us back to the difficulties that I explored in the last chapter. Who actually wields the sword? Puritan radicals like Goodman and his Scots companion-in-exile John Knox were no more willing to wait for "the people" than for the magistrates. They appealed to the faithful: "Who is on the Lord's side? let him come unto me." And then the faithful enforce the covenant against the people, in the name of the people themselves. It should be clear by now, however, that the covenantal argument can make for a different and a more democratic kind of politics: public commitment, instruction, prophetic complaint, and public recommitment. The whole process is founded on the moral competence of ordinary men and women and constitutes a slow forward movement (despite popular backsliding and kingly corruption). And then, the vanguard of the faithful must always wait for the agreement of the people. Josiah's reformation is a useful model, for the reading of the law and the renewal of the covenant comes first and the repression of "idolatrous priests" and the ritual defilement of the "high places" (2 Kings 23:2–14) only afterward. Reformation is inspired by zealous individuals, committed to the covenant, but that very commitment requires them, before marching into battle with God at their head, to seek the people's consent to their wars. As contemporary theologians of liberation argue, the covenant (and, they would say, the gospel, too) requires not only that we take a stand against oppression but that we do so in "authentic solidarity" with the oppressed.[34]

I V

THE COVENANT is an event set within the larger process of deliverance, a crucial feature of the Exodus pattern. Like the pattern as a whole, it is self-consciously reenacted by later generations of Bible readers. More than any other part of the pattern, however, the covenant is an explicit incitement to action. "You are committed: now do what God requires." It must sometimes have surprised men and women who had never stood, even in imagination, at the foot of Sinai (or in any similar place) to be told that they wore the Lord's collar. The claim fits more easily into a determinist than a voluntarist argument. But when the people engage themselves again—it doesn't matter whether they are repeating an event in their own history or in someone else's history—they make themselves into free men and women. Having committed themselves, of course, they are in an important sense unfree, bound to obey the law. Since they have bound themselves, how-ever, they are *freely bound.*

Nor is it impossible to break the law, as they will quickly learn. God's taskmasters are not like Pharaoh's; they give the people more leeway. And the conventional "leaders" of the people are themselves more likely to disobey the commandments and to encourage (or even require) disobedience than to imitate the ways of Moses. The rich and the powerful are corrupt, and the people are weak, and soon they find themselves sliding back toward Egyptian decadence and slavery. Thus the Exodus history of the Book of Nehemiah:

> Neither have our kings, our princes, our priests, our fa-thers, kept thy law, nor hearkened unto thy command-ments and thy testimonies [Hebrew *'edoth,* "pacts"]. . . . Behold we are servants [slaves] this day, and for the land that thou gavest unto our fathers . . . we are servants [slaves] in it.   (9:34, 36)

But these slaves are also men and women freely bound to God. And so they can be drawn into the hard work of deliverance in a way that the original slaves in Egypt were never drawn in. In the time of Ezra and Nehemiah, this meant renewing the covenant and then rebuilding the political and religious community. In other times, the hard work of deliverance has extended to radical and oppositional politics—even a politics directed against kings, princes, priests, and fathers.

Such a politics is by no means disinterested. It is not the case that the people fulfill the covenant for the sake of the covenant, do their duty because duty ought to be done. They fulfill the covenant for the sake of God's promises. When they decide to resume the march, it is because they are marching toward the promised land. We must now ask what (and where) the promised land is.

FOUR

The Promised Land

ARGUED in the first chapter of this book that the end of the Exodus story, the promised land, was present at the beginning as a hope and an aspiration: without that there could have been no beginning. The hard question in stories of this sort is whether the end is present at the end. Do the children of Israel reach the promised land? Well, yes, they do; though the land was rosier in the promising than in the getting. Or, better, the promise turned out to have qualifying clauses. The land would never be all that it could be until its new inhabitants were all that they should be. The promise, in fact, had a complex twofold character: God said, "I will bring you into a land flowing with milk and honey," and He also said, "Ye shall be unto me a kingdom of priests and a holy nation." The land is the opposite of Egyptian bondage: free farming instead of slave labor (in Deuteronomy 11, freedom and slavery are associated with rain and irrigation respectively—a distant source, perhaps, of Karl Wittfogel's argument that oriental despotism has its origin in the control of the water supply[1]). The kingdom is the opposite of Egyptian corruption: holiness instead of idolatry. Both these promises require human cooperation. God brings the Israelites out of Egypt, but they themselves must make the trek across the desert and conquer Canaan and work the land. And God gives the Israelites laws, which they must learn to live by. Since the laws are never fully observed, the land is never completely possessed. Canaan becomes Israel, and still remains a *promised* land.

The twofold character of the promise seems to fit well with what I have called the Leninist reading of the text. In his theory of revolution, Lenin identified two forms of consciousness, the first belonging to the mass of workers, the second to the vanguard; and he argued that these forms of consciousness give rise to two political goals, the first focused on a better life (trade unionism), the second on a new society (socialism).[2] One can make out a similar dualism in the Exodus; indeed, this is a common interpretation of the Exodus and though it isn't usually expressed in a Leninist idiom, it easily could be. The promise of milk and honey speaks to the consciousness of the slaves in Egypt. That's why the promise is announced by Moses (actually, by Aaron on Moses' behalf) immediately upon his return to Egypt, early in the story (Exod. 4:30). It represents the hope of the slaves for a share of what their masters already have, but in a place of their own, where they will be neither slaves nor strangers. Milk and honey is their spontaneous desire: as their lives were made bitter by Pharaoh, so they hope for a little sweetness. The promise of holiness, by contrast, speaks to the consciousness of Moses himself and of the elect group that gathers around him in the wilderness. That's why the promise is delivered in the wilderness, after the "going out" from Egypt (Exod. 19:5–6). Holiness is the political and religious theory of the Mosaic vanguard, who teach it to the people and defend it, when necessary, against the people. It expresses the vanguard's rejection of everything Egyptian and its vision of how Israel ought to live in the promised land. Though the phrase "a kingdom of priests and a holy nation" provides no geographical reference, it has a temporal reference. The promising verbs in Exodus 19 are future/conditional. They can refer to the immediate future: if, *right now,* you obey My voice and keep My covenant, you shall be, *now,* a kingdom of priests. In fact, however, obedience is a struggle that extends over many years; holiness lies ahead in time as Canaan does in space.

The people, dreaming of milk and honey, are materialists; Moses and the Levites, dreaming of holiness, are idealists. This is the standard interpretation of the murmurings and, more generally, of the political struggles of the wilderness period. But the standard interpretation has a political purpose: it upholds the position of Moses and the Levites. The people see and want; Moses has a vision and a program. Or, to adopt now the idiom of Christian accounts, the people have carnal desires, while Moses, a prototype of Christ, glimpses a spiritual end that he cannot yet reveal (or which the people cannot yet understand). The promises and prophecies, writes Pascal, "have a hidden and spiritual meaning to which this people were hostile, under the carnal meaning which they loved. If the spiritual meaning had been revealed, they would not have loved it."[3] I would rather say—this is a Jewish account— that the "spiritual" meaning was revealed, and some of the people, at least, loved it well enough. Holiness had its advocates, even its zealots. The tensions produced by the twofold character of the promise are plainly visible in the text. But there is something wrong with the account of these tensions in terms of a simple opposition between materialism and idealism, carnal and spiritual meanings, spontaneous politics and high theory. There is, if I may say so, an idealism, a spirituality, a high theory of milk and honey; and it is easy to see—indeed, it is suggested in the text—that the Levites have a material interest in holiness. We need to look at each of these, and at some of their historical repetitions and enactments, more carefully.

II

THE PROMISE of milk and honey is endlessly elaborated, first in those biblical texts, most importantly Deuteronomy and the Prophets, that reflect upon the Exodus, and then in later religious and political interpretations. The earliest readings are simply expansions. Thus Moses, in one of his Deuteronomic sermons to the people:

> For the Lord thy God bringeth thee into a good land, a land of brooks of water, of fountains and depths that spring out of valleys and hills. A land of wheat and barley, and vines, and fig trees, and pomegranates; a land of oil, olive, and honey. A land wherein thou shalt eat bread without scarceness, thou shalt not lack anything in it.   (Deut. 8:-7–9)

It is interesting that Moses, even at this late date (he is speaking shortly before his own death and the crossing of Israel into Canaan), doesn't promise to fill the fleshpots, as if he is still unwilling to make that last concession to popular desire. Still, his meaning is clear enough: milk and honey stand for material plenitude; the words evoke and are meant to evoke a picture of a land where the living is easy. But this picture is subject to further expansion. A land without scarcity is also a land without oppression; the pastoral and agricultural imagery of the original promise is easily given a moral turn, as in the words of comfort spoken by the prophets. One of Isaiah's visions of the new Jerusalem provides a nice example:

> And [my people] shall build houses and inhabit them; and they shall plant vineyards, and eat the fruit of them. They shall not build and another inhabit; they shall not plant and another eat.   (65:21–22)

Here the prophet is probably addressing the exiles in Babylonia; he assures them that one day they will live again in the promised land, and this time without the fear of foreign conquest. But his words also suggest that they will be free from domestic bondage. In the new Jerusalem there won't be cruel taskmasters who seize what the people produce: they shall "enjoy the work of their hands. They shall not labor in vain" (65:22–23). Isaiah's vision still plays against the memory of Egypt—though now there are other memories, more recent oppressions.

So it isn't only a matter of "flesh to eat . . . cucumbers and melons . . . garlic and onions." The promise to the people reaches farther than that, for the people also dream of justice and freedom. In their minds (as in ours), the material and the ideal, the carnal and the spiritual are not so easily separated. Again and again in the history of popular struggles, these opposites appear together. Consider, for example, the words of a radical pamphleteer during the English Revolution, who describes Canaan as "a land of large liberty, the house of happiness where, like the Lord's lily, [the children of Israel] toil not but grow in a land flowing with sweet wine, milk and honey . . .

without money."[4] "Happiness" sounds like a characteristically modern version of the promise; it is a little odd to imagine the Israelites marching across the desert in pursuit of happiness. But that is only because the word, as we understand it, is a little too weak. Miserable in Egypt, the people were indeed promised joy in Canaan. "And there ye shall eat before the Lord your God, and ye shall rejoice in all that ye put your hand unto . . . " (Deut. 12:7). "Joy" and "gladness" are common descriptions of life in the promised land—and then in this or that postrevolutionary society. Perhaps happiness is simply the secularized version of religious joy. In any case, the word is used, not only in the Declaration of Independence but also in the Exodus sermons of the 1770s and 1780s, to describe the goal of the American Revolution.[5] (The parallel word, which corresponds to holiness as happiness does to milk and honey, is "virtue.") I have to say, however, that the notion of a land without money has no biblical sources; it is a modern (or perhaps a late medieval) invention. But it is not an entirely implausible elaboration of the ideas of justice and abundance, and it has a long afterlife.

In Latin America today, Catholic priests who have read Marx as well as the Bible describe the promised land as a society free at last from "exploitation." They explicitly reject Pascal's insistence on the mere carnality of milk and honey. Thus Gutierrez:

> In this statement [of Pascal's] . . . there is an assumption which should be brought to the surface, namely a certain idea of the spiritual characterized by a kind of [dualism]. . . . This is a disincarnate "spiritual," scornfully superior to all earthly realities. The proper way to pose the question does not seem to us to be in terms of "temporal promise or spiritual promise." Rather . . . it is a matter of partial fulfillments through liberating historical events.

The carnal or temporal promise has an ethical meaning, which derives from the fact that it was delivered to slaves. "It presupposes the defense of the rights of the poor, punishment of oppressors, a life free from the fear of being enslaved by others. . . . " To neglect or devalue these aspects of milk and honey in the name of the spirit is to misunderstand the spirit. "The elimination of misery and exploitation," Gutierrez goes on, "is a sign of the coming of the Kingdom."[6] This is also, I think, the prophetic view of the first Exodus promise, and it can't be reduced, in Leninist terms, to the "trade unionism" of the oppressed. The door of hope opens on a larger vision, not simply of more and more of whatever good things are available but of enough for everyone. Then everyone will be secure in his possessions, and there won't be any tyrants in the land. "They shall sit every man under his vine and under his fig tree; and none shall make them afraid" (Mic. 4:4).

III

BUT one can imagine a Levitical objection to all this: that it makes liberation seem too easy, as if it is just a matter of escaping from Egypt, arriving in Canaan; as if there is some magic in the promised land itself. There are indeed tendencies in Jewish thought that we might think of as territorialist—suggestions that merely living on the land is a good thing and a guarantee of blessings.[7] But the deeper argument of the Exodus story is that righteousness is the only guarantee. And this, too, is the argument of the prophets, who stress not only the larger meaning of milk and honey but also the radical conditionality of the Sinai covenant. "If ye be willing and obedient," says Isaiah, "ye shall eat the good of the land" (1:19). And if not, not. For Moses and the Levites, the primary goal of the Exodus is the founding of "a kingdom of priests and a holy nation." Only for such a nation will the promised land fulfill its promise. Bring slaves into Canaan, and Canaan will soon become another Egypt. Of course, God promised that Israel would be holy, but He didn't promise that it would be holy tomorrow or next Tuesday or even at the end of forty years. Conceived in territorialist terms, the promise of milk and honey has a temporal end point: sooner or later, the people will cross the Jordan and enter the land. Conceived in ethical terms, the promise is temporally uncertain, for its achievement is not a matter of where we plant our feet but of how we cultivate our spirits. Once again, the contrast is too sharp; the march through the desert and the conquest of the land themselves require spiritedness and solidarity. The transformation of the mob of slaves into a disciplined (holy) nation is a political as well as a religious necessity. And so the maxim *no milk and honey without obedience to God* is politically as well as religiously plausible. Still, it makes a difference whether one emphasizes the milk and honey or the divine commandments.

What is the meaning of "a kingdom of priests and a holy nation"? The second promise is closely tied to the first or, at least, to the extended version of the first—tied in an obvious and then in a complex way. What is required of a holy nation is that its members obey divine law, and much of that law is concerned with the rejection of Egyptian bondage. In such a nation, then, no one would oppress a stranger, or deny Sabbath rest to his servants, or withhold the wages of a worker. A kingdom of priests would be a kingdom without a king (God would be king); hence it would be without pharaohs and without taskmasters. There would be no one with the power to "take . . . your goodliest young men . . . and put them to his work." The prophets, defending the idea of a holy nation, repeatedly denounce political tyranny and social injustice; once again, these two are hard to separate. I needn't quote any passages: these are probably the most familiar parts of the Bible. I would only stress again the way in which the prophetic denunciations play against the background of the Exodus, endlessly reiterating the images of bondage and deliverance. The memory of Egypt is a crucial feature of the new national consciousness.[8]

So the two promises come together: if no member of the holy nation is an oppressor, then no inhabitant of the promised land will be oppressed. But there is more to be said about the second promise. "A kingdom of priests and a holy nation" is the original version, and one of the key sources, of a whole series of revolutionary programs: the Puritan holy commonwealth, the Jacobin republic of virtue, even Lenin's communist society. None of these is adequately characterized by the negative ideal of nonoppression. In none of them is it enough for men to sit happily under their vines and their fig trees. They all require an active and lively participation in religious and-/or political life, and they require this not from some of the people but from all of them. The promise of milk and honey involves a kind of negative egalitarianism: it works against the gross inequalities of tyrant and subject, taskmaster and slave. The second promise aims at positive equality. In God's kingdom, all the Israelites will be priests; the nation as a whole will be holy. Hence the establishment of the Levitical priesthood after "the people's sin with the calf" was a defeat for revolutionary aspiration. It is not quite like going back to Egypt—at least it's not described in those terms—for the achievement of the kingdom is only postponed, not given up. One rabbinic commentary suggests that the kingdom actually existed briefly, between the covenant and the calf. During that time every Israelite (or perhaps only every firstborn Israelite) had the privileges of a priest; afterward, the privileges were restricted to the Levites and the sons of Aaron.[9]

Once that restriction is in place, the second promise opens the way for a new kind of opposition to Moses and his immediate followers. Consider for a moment the example of Eldad and Medad in Numbers 11. By this time, the tabernacle has stood for some months outside the camp, and religious revelation is delivered only from there, with Moses himself presiding.

> But there remained two men in the camp . . . Eldad and Medad . . . and they prophesied in the camp. And there ran a young man and told Moses, and said, Eldad and Medad do prophesy in the camp. And Joshua, the son of Nun, the servant of Moses . . . answered and said, My lord Moses, forbid them. And Moses said unto him, Enviest thou for my sake? would God that all the Lord's people were prophets. (11:26–29)

Moses remembers the promise, though Joshua has already forgotten it. Or, Joshua is concerned above all, despite the promise, to maintain the fragile authority of the new religious and political leadership.[10] In the event, Eldad and Medad are allowed to prophesy, and independent prophecy remains a permanent, if often a precarious, feature of Israel's religious life. But the new leadership prevails, as Joshua wanted it to, and it prevails for a long time. Moses' hope is transformed by the prophet Joel into a vision of the messianic age:

And it shall come to pass afterward, that I will pour out my spirit upon all flesh; and your sons and your daughters shall prophesy, your old men shall dream dreams, your young men shall see visions; And also upon the servants and upon the handmaids . . . will I pour out my spirit. (2:28–29)

The whole nation, sons and daughters, old and young, masters and servants, will be holy *afterward;* meanwhile, however, there are priests and prophets who claim authority over their fellows. How can that claim be justified? This is the question posed by the rebel Korah: "Ye take too much upon you," he says to Moses and Aaron, "seeing all the congregation is holy, every one of them. . . . Wherefore then lift ye up yourselves above the congregation of the Lord?" (Num. 16:3). Korah is the first left oppositionist in the history of radical politics. (The rabbinic elaborations of Korah's argument stress his radicalism and indeed make him into a social and economic as well as a political rebel.[11]) Moses doesn't reply in the text, but it is easy to imagine what he would have said. His whole experience, in Egypt and in the wilderness, forced upon him a powerful sense of the people's unholiness. Despite the covenant, Israel had still to become holy: "ye shall be. . . . " And that would require a long and painful struggle. Korah had experienced the great moment of deliverance and the enthusiasm of the original covenanting not as a promise of what might be in the far future but as an immediate reality. Thus the midrashic interpretation of his complaint to Moses and Aaron:

All the congregation are holy, every one of them, and they have all heard at Sinai the commandment: I am the Lord thy God (Exodus 20:2): *Wherefore then lift ye up yourselves? . . .* If you alone had heard it, while they had not, you could have claimed superiority. But . . . now they have all heard it.[12]

Everyone was holy who had shared the Sinai experience, and so there was no need for a leader or a priesthood. But that, Moses would have argued, makes holiness too easy, like milk and honey. In fact, it is a hard business. We might worry, though, that it was now in the interests of the Levites to make it even harder than it was.

Many centuries later, Protestantism renewed the promise of universal priesthood and universal prophecy, and John Milton, writing his *Areopagitica* in the early years of the Puritan revolution, thought that the moment of fulfillment had finally arrived. "For now the time seems come, wherein Moses the great Prophet may sit in heaven rejoicing to see that memorable and glorious wish of his fulfilled, when . . . all the Lord's people are become prophets."[13] All that seemed necessary in 1644 was to set the people free from the "fretting" (Milton's word) of men like Joshua. Seven years later, when Cromwell returned to the argument, things looked rather more difficult. Opening the first session of the parliament of saints, Cromwell felt compelled to explain why the members had been appointed rather than elected, "called" by himself rather than by "the suffrage of the people." Surely election would be better, he said. "None can desire it more than I! Would that all the Lord's people were prophets. I would all were fit to be called." But they aren't fit, not yet, and the "likeliest way to bring them to their liberties" is that "men fearing God do now rule them in the fear of God."[14] Moses would probably have said the same thing.

One could trace a similar history in the case of the French Revolution, though probably without the Exodus references. The original promise of the revolution (after the promise of bread) was that everyone would share, and share equally, in the required religious or political performances. But it turned out again that some were called and others not. The Jacobin clubs produced a priesthood of virtuous citizens. Perhaps the only way to avoid such a priesthood is to reduce the rigor of the required performances, to make holiness and virtue less troublesome than men like Cromwell and Robespierre believed them to be. I suppose that this is the democratic way, at least it is one democratic way, to fulfill the second promise. Perhaps it is the American way. I found a nice example of it in a lecture delivered to the students of Yale University in 1902 by David Brewer, a justice of the United States Supreme Court. The voting booth, Brewer said,

> is the temple of American institutions. No single tribe or family is chosen to watch the sacred fires. . . . Each of us is a priest. To each is given the care of the ark of the covenant. Each one ministers at its altars.[15]

And all we have to do is vote! But America at the turn of the century seems an unlikely example of "a kingdom of priests and a holy nation." It looks more like a case of a people living in the promised land but sliding back into Egyptian practices—exactly like the first Israel.

IV

THE ISRAELITES crossed the Jordan and found themselves, soon enough, back in Egypt. Of course, the original promise was fulfilled, but it was fulfilled the way promises are fulfilled in history, not in myth. I am reminded of

Thomas Mann's account of Joseph interpreting Pharaoh's dream and predicting seven full years and seven lean years. Of course, says Mann, the prediction was realized, but the seven full years, if truth be told, were more like five, and of those five, two were not much fuller (though they certainly weren't any leaner) than average years . . . .[16] So the land of Canaan did not exactly flow with milk and honey, but there was milk and honey, and flesh to fill the pots. The extended meaning of the promise—the end of oppression—that was more problematic. Pharaoh reappeared in Moabite and Philistine form and then in Israelite form. "The Egyptian overseers," writes Ernst Bloch, "had merely changed their names; they still sat there in the Israelite towns."[17]

The textual explanation for the new oppression is simple and straightforward: "The children of Israel did evil in the sight of the Lord." This is the reiterated theme of the Book of Judges (see, for example, 3:7,12 and 4:1), connecting the military successes of Israel's enemies to the people's repeated lapses into idolatry. The prophets make a larger argument: the oppression of Israelites by foreigners finds its deepest cause in the oppression of Israelites by one another. The argument is briefly and sharply put in the first chapter of Lamentations: "Judah is gone into captivity because of affliction, and because of great servitude" (1:3, repeating the Exodus words). We can fill in the details from Isaiah and Jeremiah. The people turned to idol worship, to the fetishism of material things, then to material things themselves, then to Egyptian luxuries. They forsook the commandments, forgot that they had been slaves—and then they (or some of them) oppressed the poor. And when they felt guilty about the oppression, they came back to God with sacrifices and they fasted in contrition: for a day at a time, they gave up milk and honey. But God's eye, according to the prophets, is focused on the whole of the chain of evil, and what He requires, even in the promised land, is a new deliverance. Thus Isaiah:

> Is not this the fast that I have chosen? to loose the bands of wickedness, to undo the heavy burdens, and to let the oppressed go free, and that ye break every yoke? (58:6)

As Pharaoh forgot Joseph, so now the Israelites have forgotten Egypt—and to forget Egypt means to forget the God who delivered them out of Egypt, and to forget the divine deliverance is to return to Egyptian oppression. This is the prophetic version of Santayana's maxim that those who cannot remember the past are condemned to repeat it. And if the oppression is repeated, so must the liberation be.

So the two promises are connected again, in a more complex fashion. Holiness makes for liberty and justice, but it is effective only insofar as it describes a way of life, a religious and political culture. The Israelites will not be a holy nation until they are, all of them, participants in a world of ritual remembering; until they celebrate the Passover, rest on the Sabbath, study the law; until they actively "break every yoke" and learn to live with what Bloch calls the "ineradicable subversion" of the Exodus story.[18] This is God's kingdom and, in some ultimate sense, every place else is Egypt.

V

THE DISCOVERY of Egypt in Canaan generates a series of reinterpretations of the Exodus. The first of these and the strangest (though we have seen it since) involves what might best be called a romanticizing of the wilderness period. The prophets Hosea and Jeremiah are the leading romantics. For them the ethical high point of the Exodus is not the arrival in Canaan but the march across the desert. More exactly, it is the beginning of the march. The people's commitment to God was never stronger than at that wonderful moment when they chose Him and followed Him "into a land of deserts and pits." "I remember," Jeremiah has God saying to Israel, "the kindness of thy youth, the love of thine espousals when thou wentest after me in the wilderness" (2:2). Youth and love are the symbols here of religious purity and zeal. Hosea imagines God seducing Israel, hoping to rekindle that zeal:

> Therefore, behold, I will allure her, and bring her into the wilderness, and speak comfortably unto her . . . and the valley of Achor [shall be] for a door of hope: and she shall sing there, as in the days of her youth, and as in the day when she came up out of the land of Egypt. (3:14–15)

Forgotten here is the fearfulness of the people at the sea and their ceaseless murmuring in the desert. For Hosea, the crucial point is the willingness of the Israelites, not their hesitations and anxieties. And many radicals since have made the same point: the moral climax of the revolution comes at the beginning of the revolution, when oppressed men and women take their first steps toward freedom.[19] There is only trouble after that, but at least this is self-made trouble, not the affliction of slaves.

The prophet in the promised land recalls the original moment of deliverance and hopes to recapture and prolong it. But this invites in turn a new interpretation of the promise. However wonderful the first days of freedom were, no one in his right mind would march into the wilderness without the hope of a "good land" on the other side. But how can that land be described once one is already there and disappointed? I should say immediately that this is not a permanent problem, since the people are not, as it turns out, permanently settled in the land. Writing after the exile of the northern tribes or during the years of the Babylonian captivity, the prophets can describe a new Exodus to the same place. The place has a new name now; it is Israel, not Canaan, but it is still a land of milk and honey and of all the further contentments that milk and honey signify. The promise is repeated, its fulfillment postponed: the true and final possession of the land is still to come. The first deliverance was incomplete, or it was repudiated when the people "corrupted themselves" in the promised land just as they had done at the holy mountain. But there would be a second deliverance, greater than the first. So Jeremiah consoled the people of the southern kingdom:

> Therefore, behold, the days come, saith the Lord, that they shall no more say, the Lord liveth which brought up the children of Israel out of the land of Egypt; But, the Lord liveth which brought up and which led the seed of the house of Israel out of the north country, and from all countries whither I had driven them; and they shall dwell in their own land.   (23:7–8)

Jewish messianic thought, and so all messianic thought, has its origins in this idea of a second Exodus. The idea is soon entangled, in ways I shall not try to explain, with elements of the royalist ideology of the house of David, and the future leader of the redemption comes to be described more often in kingly than in prophetic terms.[20] For now I want only to stress that the postponement of the promise is one way of dealing with its (temporary) failure.

The postponement is a rebuke to the people, but a rebuke that holds open the door of hope. If they repent and reform their conduct, they will yet enjoy the milk and honey of the land; they will yet be, all of them, priests in God's kingdom. The promise doesn't change in the promised land. Under conditions that represent the culmination of "backsliding"—oppression at home and then a new captivity—the prophets simply reiterate the terms of the Sinai covenant. They represent the conscience of the revolution.

But there are alternative ways of dealing with failure, alternatives that are often tried out, as it were, in the same books from which I have just been quoting. As the promise is postponed, so it is also elaborated, heightened, and ultimately transformed. It loses its precise historical and geographical dimensions, but it shines all the more brightly in mental space. The promise becomes utopian. Let me give a relatively restrained but nonetheless revealing example of this process before I turn to some of its more extravagant outcomes. In Jeremiah 31, the prophet promises the people not only a new Exodus but also a new covenant—and a covenant significantly different from the original one:

> Behold, the days come, saith the Lord, that I will make a new covenant with the house of Israel. . . . Not according to the covenant that I made with their fathers in the day that I took them by the hand to bring them out of the land of Egypt; which . . . covenant they broke. . . . But this shall be the covenant that I will make with the house of Israel; after those days, saith the Lord, I will put my law in their inward parts, and write it in their hearts. . . . And they shall teach no more every man his neighbor and every man his brother, saying, Know the Lord: for they shall all know me, from the least of them unto the greatest of them. (31:31–34)

This is a remarkable passage, not least because it suggests the possibility of a messianic age without a messiah. Though the prophet uses Exodus imagery, he makes Moses superfluous—not only as a teacher but also as a political leader, for that line about teaching every man his neighbor and every man his brother echoes the Mosaic command of Exodus 32 about killing every man his neighbor and every man his brother. It won't be necessary to teach for the same reason that it won't be necessary to kill: because the people will willingly and wholeheartedly obey the law. God will make vanguard consciousness into the natural or spontaneous consciousness of ordinary men and women.

The original covenant was delivered to the ears of the people, and its terms, as I have emphasized, were conditional: "if ye will obey my voice . . . ye shall be unto me a kingdom of priests . . ." (Exod. 19:5–6). The new covenant bypasses the ears; it is inscribed in the hearts of the people, and so the if/then conditionalism is no longer relevant; there can be no disobedience. What Jeremiah promises, in effect, is a transformation of human nature or, better, the reappearance of the original Adam—a little out of place, I should think, in the land of deserts and pits. And then it is but a short and obvious step to bring him home, to make the goal of the second Exodus not Canaan but Eden. This is the crucial move in the development of a full-fledged messianism out of Exodus thinking. Once this move is made, the Exodus can be reinterpreted, first in Jewish apocalyptic literature and then in Christian writings, as an allegory for the final redemption of mankind. In both cases, though more emphatically and insistently in the Christian tradition, the allegorical reading tends to override all historical distinctions. "The Garden of Eden, the Promised Land, Jerusalem, and Mount Zion," writes Northrop Frye, "are interchangeable synonyms for the home of the soul, and in Christian imagery they are all identical . . . with the kingdom of God spoken of by Jesus."[21] If we attend to Exodus history, of course, they are not identical at all, for (to take only the first two) Eden is a mythical garden while the promised land has latitude and longitude; Eden stands at the beginning and then, in messianic thought, at the very end of human history, while the promised land is firmly located within history; and Eden represents the perfection of nature and human nature, while the promised land is simply a better place than Egypt was.

So messianism derives from the Exodus but stands radically apart from it. Not only is the messianic promise unconditional, as Saadya Gaon argued, but its content is utterly new. Freed from the specific opposition to Egypt, the picture of "the new heaven and the new earth" is worked out, instead, in opposition to this world, this life. It is not hard bondage but daily trouble, not the "evil diseases" of Egypt but disease itself, that will vanish when the messiah comes. History will stop—an idea entirely alien to the Exodus texts, which almost seem designed to teach that the promises will never definitively be fulfilled, that backsliding and struggle are permanent features of human existence.[22] And even if the promises were fulfilled, the result would still be a holy community living in historical time, its citizens farming the land, waiting for the rain, watching for foreign enemies, celebrating the seventh day and the seventh year and the jubilee. The end of days is a new idea.

I am not going to dwell on the Last Days. According to both Jewish and Christian apocalyptic writings, they will be preceded by terrible catastrophes—persecutions, wars, floods, and earthquakes; great "shakings" of the kingdoms of the world and of the world itself. So frightening is the prospect of the days before the Last Days that there is a saying about the messiah recorded in the Talmud, attributed to three different rabbis of the third and fourth centuries: "May he come, but I do not want to see him."[23] The vivid accounts of upheaval and destruction play a significant part later on in the politics of medieval millenarianism. Indeed, I would venture to suggest that the apocalypse is to millenarian and chiliastic radicalism what the Exodus is to revolutionary politics. Taborites, Anabaptists, Ranters—the groups that figure in Norman Cohn's *Pursuit of the Millennium*—draw their inspiration from a literature that entirely lacks the tough realism of the Exodus story.[24] To be sure, there are men and women who move back and forth between Exodus and apocalypse, but the lines are generally clear. It is one thing to hope for milk and honey, or even for holiness, and it is something quite different to try (what the rabbis, after the failure of the Bar Kochba revolt, commanded Jews never to try) "to force the End," to bring mankind suddenly and violently into the messianic age, the new Jerusalem, Paradise itself.

For it is Paradise, not the promised land, Eden, not Canaan, that lies just on the other side of the next-to-Last Days. Here is a description from the Syriac Book of Baruch, one of the apocryphal or meta-apocryphal books (it was excluded from the Christian Apocrypha), which dates from the first century but draws heavily on Isaiah:

> And then healing shall descend in
>   dew,
> And disease shall withdraw,
> And anxiety and anguish and
>   lamentation pass from among men,
> And gladness proceed through the
>   whole earth;

And no one shall again die
   untimely,
Nor shall any adversity suddenly
   befall.

. . . .

And wild beasts shall come from the
   forest and minister unto men,
And asps and vipers shall come
   forth from their holes to submit
   themselves to a little child;
And women shall no longer have pain
   when they bear,
Nor shall they suffer torment when
   they yield the fruit of the
   womb.[25]

And so on; I omit other wonderful things, not out of any
lack of appreciation. These are promises better than any of
the promises delivered in Egypt or in the wilderness. But
they do not invite anything like the ongoing human effort
required in the Exodus story: marching across the desert,
teaching, learning, obeying the law. Messianic radicalism
sometimes required its zealots to join in the shakings of the
political kingdoms, to root out and destroy corruption
wherever they found it. After that, however, they had
only to wait for the divine transformation of the ruined
world. The Exodus suggested a very different program.

VI

AMONG both Jews and Christians there was strong resistance to messianic politics—resistance that took characteristically different forms. Christian writers tended to

spiritualize the Last Days and to describe redemption as a state of the soul, not of the world. Jews tended to return to the Exodus (or to some combination of Exodus thinking and Davidic ideology). For them redemption always retained, and retains still, its political character.[26] That is why Christian revolutionaries, like the English Puritans or today's liberation theologians, are plausibly called judaizers: they defend the "carnality" of the promise; they seek a worldly kingdom. The dominant Jewish view (though I don't doubt the strength of popular apocalypticism) is given by the Babylonian teacher Samuel in the third century; his sentence is frequently repeated in rabbinic writings. "There is no difference between this world and the Days of the Messiah, except our bondage to the heathen kingdoms."[27] As Gershom Scholem has emphasized, this is a polemical remark, aimed at all those teachers and writers who hoped for a return to Eden. The only return will be to Canaan; messianic redemption repeats the Mosaic redemption; it is a deliverance from bondage. Writing in the thirteenth century, Nachmanides described this deliverance as a literal repetition of the Exodus: "The Messiah . . . will come [to Rome] and command the Pope and all the kings of the nations in the name of God, 'Let my people go that they may serve Me.' "[28]

The greatest of medieval Jewish philosophers argued in much the same way. The messiah, according to Maimonides, will be a human and historical figure, exactly as Moses and David were, and the world into which he comes will "continue in its accustomed course." Isaiah's prophecy about the wolf and the lamb, repeated by Baruch and many other apocalyptic writers, is "a parable and an allegory which must be understood to mean that Israel will dwell securely even among the . . . heathen nations." Maimonides goes on to offer a picture of the messianic age that can be understood in part as a rabbinic elaboration of the Exodus promises—and perhaps because of that a rather modest, though also a lovely, vision of the future.

> The sages and prophets longed for the days of the Messiah not in order to rule over the world and not to bring the heathen under their control, not to be exalted of the nations, or even to eat, drink, and rejoice. All they wanted was to have time for the Torah and its wisdom with no one to oppress or disturb them. In that age . . . the whole world will be occupied . . . with the knowledge of God . . . [and] the children of Israel will be great sages; they will know hidden things and attain an understanding of their Creator to the extent of human capability.[29]

The kingdom of priests is replaced here by a kingdom of rabbis—scholars and sages—and the form of participation is study. The vision is resolutely anti-apocalyptic; "the extent of human capability" sets a limit on what we can expect; our understanding of God will be neither pure nor perfect. At the same time, I have to stress that this isn't simply an elaboration of the Exodus promises; it is also an enlargement, a heightening. The Babylonian captivity, the destruction of the two temples, the centuries of exile and persecution have had the effect of raising the stakes of Exodus history. Maimonides dreams of a greater and, finally, a definitive redemption.

His is still, however, an uneasy messianism. One of his followers argued that if only the Jews were sages and scholars already, all of them, the messiah would be unnecessary. "Would that all God's people were prophets," wrote Rabbi Isaac ben Yedaiah, "wise enough to know their Creator, so that they would not need any king other than our God, the King of kings."[30] This repeats Moses' wish and suggests that for some of the rabbis, at least, the messiah, like the Levitical priesthood, was an unfortunate necessity, his role determined by the moral or spiritual backsliding of the people and not by God's original plan. Without messianic leadership, Israel would never reach the promised land. Once there, however, the people will come into their own; they will be priests and prophets or sages and scholars (in secular versions of the argument, they will be republican citizens), and princely power will no longer be required.

But that is to say, once they are *really* there, the people will come into their own, all of them will be sages, and they will have no need of a king. For when they were there before, after the original deliverance, the people insisted that they did need a king. They came to Samuel —the incident is much discussed in the political theory of kingship—and asked in effect for an Israelite pharaoh to judge them and lead them into battle; they wanted to be "like all the nations." Samuel complained to God, who told him to give the people what they wanted, "for they have not rejected thee, but they have rejected me, that I should not reign over them" (1 Sam. 8:5,7). And then Samuel found them a king, just as Aaron had built them an idol. These are the two great refusals of the "kingdom of priests and the holy nation," and each one is abetted by God's chosen servant—a sign perhaps that the kingdom must wait upon the people's will. God insists upon His heavenly but not upon His earthly kingship (would He be a tyrant if He ruled without the people's consent?). Nor, most of the rabbis agree, will He send the messiah until the people are ready to receive him. But when they are ready, it might be said, they won't need a messiah.

These are difficult arguments, and the rabbis go round and round with them, as I have been doing too. But I will step out of the circle now and return to my political theme. The government of the promised land is to be a kingdom without a human king. This is a reiterated revolutionary vision, and though it is often betrayed, it is important nonetheless. Political leadership in the new society is in principle temporary, charismatic, consensual. There is no Leader and no hereditary line of leaders. This crucial idea is deeply embedded in the biblical text—so deeply that the editors and redactors who worked in David's and in Solomon's court never managed to get it out. Consider, for example, the last chapter of Deuteronomy, where God shows Moses the promised land, telling him at the same time that he will never enter it. Moses dies there, on the far side of the Jordan, and God buries him in a valley in the land of Moab, and "no man knoweth of his sepulchre unto this day" (34:6). The biblical sentences have been endlessly elaborated in midrashic writings,[31] but I want to focus on the text itself, which can be taken to stress the contrast between Moses and his great antagonist, the Egyptian pharaoh, whose burial place is man-made, rich and splendid, and widely known. Moses is not a king. He is not a king like Pharaoh; he is not a king-messiah; and he is not a father of kings or messiahs. Indeed, of Moses' heirs and descendants, the Bible tells us virtually nothing: there is a single fragmentary allusion to a grandson who seems to have been a minor functionary at a local shrine in the territory of Dan (Judges 18:30).[32]

The restricted role of Moses is frequently emphasized in later interpretations and applications of the Exodus, often in conjunction with a reading of Exodus 18, the first constitutional text in the story, where Jethro urges Moses to associate with himself leaders chosen from among the people, and with a reading of Numbers 11, the second constitutional text, where God commands the establishment of a council of seventy elders. In Exodus 18, Jethro tells Moses, "This thing is too heavy for thee; thou art not able to perform it thyself alone." And he then proposes to choose "rulers of thousands, and rulers of hundreds, rulers of fifties, and rulers of tens" (18:18,21). Rashi worked out the arithmetic: assuming 600,000 adult males, the Israelites would have had 82,600 "rulers."[33] Roughly fifteen percent of the men would be ruling at any given time. In Numbers 11, Moses repeats Jethro's line, ". . . it is too heavy for me." Perhaps the 82,600 are not yet in place, though we are told in the earlier passage that Moses accepted Jethro's advice. There are signs in the text of some tension between the new leadership and the tribal elders—which is what one would expect in a time of political transformation.[34] In the years of the English Revolution, several constitutional schemes were put forward based on the tens and the fifties; they would have required a vast increase in political participation and so were unacceptable to parliamentary gentlemen and lawyers.[35] This in any case was the message of the biblical text: the charismatic leader is not enough; the traditionalist structure of the tribes is not adequate to the new laws; so a new government must be worked out in the wilderness—a government for the wilderness and for the promised land as well.

What kind of government is it? Spinoza, who provides what is probably the best analysis of the constitutional texts, argued that the Israelite regime was a theocratic republic.[36] So it has figured in radical and revolutionary literature, with the emphasis more often on the republicanism than the theocracy. Even Tom Paine, in his pamphlet *Common Sense,* argues against monarchy on biblical as well as commonsensical grounds, with an extended account of Israel's early history. "The Almighty hath here entered his protest against monarchical government ...."[37] (Writing in opposition to the hereditary principle, Paine omits any mention of the Levites.) For American ministers, the Exodus texts were even more central. In a sermon preached in Hartford in 1779, James Dana insisted that what the children of Israel were instructed to "remember," above all, was "the manifest interposition of the Almighty in humbling tyrants for their sakes." Israel's government, he went on, was "a confederate republic, with Jehovah at the head."[38] Urging the ratification of the new constitution before the General Court of New Hampshire in 1788, Samuel Langdon described Israel as a republic simply, and one that looked remarkably like the regime defended against the earlier confederacy by Madison and Hamilton: it was "an example to the American states."[39]

I won't attempt to comment on these unlikely arguments. Whatever the exact shape of the Exodus regime, it was certainly antimonarchical, and that is the crucial point. Joshua makes the point in dramatic fashion when he burns the chariots and hamstrings the horses captured in the course of the conquest (Josh. 11:9). For horses and chariots, as I have said before, are both the instruments and the symbols of kingly power and tyrannical rule. One of Joshua's successors, the judge and warrior Gideon, sums up the political argument of the Exodus when he responds to a suggestion that he make himself king: "I shall not rule over you, neither shall my son rule over you: the Lord shall rule over you" (Judg. 8:23). Gideon is the distant ancestor, perhaps not so distant, of Cromwell and Washington. He stands for a politics that is coherent with, that follows naturally from, the experience of deliverance, and he suggests again the revolutionary character of that experience. It calls into question the legitimacy of princely power. After the reign of David, to be sure, opposition to kingship recedes in Israel; it is only an undercurrent, though at times a powerful undercurrent, in the prophets. Hosea, for example, links kings and idols in explaining the doom of the northern kingdom:

> They have set up kings, but not by me; they have made princes, and I knew it not; of their silver and their gold have they made them idols, that they may be cut off. (8:4)

And Isaiah even more explicitly recalls Exodus radicalism: "Woe to them that go down to Egypt for help, and stay on horses, and trust in chariots . . ." (31:1). Israel should trust in the Lord. But that is also to say that it should trust in itself, in the holy nationhood for which it was originally delivered. On this view, the messiah himself represents a defeat for the politics of the Exodus. If the people had not chosen them a captain—here, a king —back for Egypt, the messiah would not be necessary. Even now, when he comes, he will do no more than fulfill the original promises. He will not abrogate the law or the studying and teaching of the law or the government of judges and magistrates in accordance with the law. He will merely establish what the people could once have established for themselves.

Within postbiblical Judaism, the doctrine I have just expounded is a conservative doctrine, directed against the radical utopianism and antinomianism of popular apocalyptic writing and prophecy.[40] It served to underwrite the authority of the rabbis within the small, more or less autonomous, Jewish communities of the diaspora. It provided no support for an innovative politics—not, at least, until the advent of Zionism, which was sometimes a return to Exodus history and sometimes a kind of political messianism. In any case, there was little room for an innovative politics in the precarious world of medieval Jewry, and there was no chance at all of deliverance from oppression except at the hands of a king-messiah. It was in Christian, and then later in secular, cities and states that the radical potential of the Exodus was realized. The story provided its readers with an alternative to the Apocalypse, a narrative frame within which it was possible to think about oppression and liberation in this-worldly terms. It suggested—it still suggests—that there might be a great day that wasn't the Last Day.

CONCLUSION

Exodus Politics

I

SINCE late medieval or early modern times, there has existed in the West a characteristic way of thinking about political change, a pattern that we commonly impose upon events, a story that we repeat to one another. The story has roughly this form: oppression, liberation, social contract, political struggle, new society (danger of restoration). We call the whole process *revolutionary*, though the events don't make a circle unless oppression is brought back at the end; intentionally, at least, they have a strong forward movement. This isn't a story told everywhere; it isn't a universal pattern; it belongs to the West, more particularly to Jews and Christians in the West, and its source, its original version, is the Exodus of Israel from Egypt. My purpose in this book has been to retell the story in its original version, to give a reading of the Exodus that captures its political meaning—and then to reflect upon the general character and internal tensions of Exodus politics. This is not, of course, the only way of

133

reading the biblical account. It is an interpretation, and like all interpretations, it highlights some features of the account and neglects or suppresses others. But I am not reading Exodus in an idiosyncratic way. I am following a well-marked trail, moving backward from citation and commentary to primary text, from enactments to acts or, at least, to stories of acts. The Exodus may or may not be what many of its commentators thought it to be, the first revolution. But the Book of Exodus (together with the Book of Numbers) is certainly the first description of revolutionary politics.

The Exodus, or the later reading of the Exodus, fixes the pattern. And because of the centrality of the Bible in Western thought and the endless repetition of the story, the pattern has been etched deeply into our political culture. It isn't only the case that events fall, almost naturally, into an Exodus shape; we work actively to give them that shape. We complain about oppression; we hope (against all the odds of human history) for deliverance; we join in covenants and constitutions; we aim at a new and better social order. Though in attenuated form, Exodus thinking seems to have survived the secularization of political theory. Thus, when utopian socialists, most of them resolutely hostile to religion, argued about the problems of the "transitional period," they still cast their arguments in familiar terms: the forty years in the wilderness, write the Manuels in their chapter on Robert Owen, were "a deep . . . cultural memory and the death of the old generation [was] an archetypal solution."[1] (It was even a solution for "scientific" socialists like Marx or, in this century, Lincoln Steffens.) This sort of thing is never merely a matter of rhetorical convenience. Cultural patterns shape perception and analysis too. They would not endure for long, of course, if they did not accommodate a range of perceptions and analyses, if it were not possible to carry on arguments inside the structures they provide. I don't mean to defend an essentialist view of revolution or of radical politics generally. Within the frame of the Exodus story one can plausibly emphasize the mighty arm of God or the slow march of the people, the land of milk and honey or the holy nation, the purging of counterrevolutionaries or the schooling of the new generation. One can describe Egyptian bondage in terms of corruption or tyranny or exploitation. One can defend the authority of the Levites or of the tribal elders or of the rulers of tens and fifties. I would only suggest that these alternatives are themselves paradigmatic; they are *our* alternatives. In other cultures, men and women read other books, tell different stories, confront different choices.

But we in the West also have a second way of talking about political change, a second pattern, the intellectual offspring, as it were, of the Exodus, though unlike it in crucial respects. The second pattern is, in Jacob Talmon's phrase, "political messianism."[2] Messianism is the great temptation of Western politics. Its source and spur is the apparent endlessness of the Exodus march. "The long drawn-out tale of human progress is shadowed by error and catastrophe," wrote the young Ramsay MacDonald in a book called *The Socialist Movement*, "by wearisome journeys in the wilderness, by Canaans which, when yet lands beyond the Jordan, were overflowing with milk and honey, but which, when conquered, were almost barren . . . ."[3] MacDonald professed himself bound to continue the march, but one might well decide to give it up (as he eventually did)—or, alternatively, to opt for a far more radical hope. Why be content with the difficult and perhaps interminable struggle for holiness and justice when there is another promised land where liberation is final, fulfillment complete? History itself is a burden from which we long to escape, and messianism guarantees that escape: a deliverance not only from Egypt but from Sinai and Canaan, too. It may seem odd to expect such a deliverance from politics—even from revolutionary politics and apocalyptic wars. Theological or philosophical arguments in defense of that expectation are always complex, invoking divine purpose or history's providential course along with this or that political program, just as the Book of Exodus does. What is important here, however, is that the messianic program is very different from the one adopted by Moses in the wilderness and at Sinai.

II

IN Jewish history this difference is somewhat muted because messianism itself takes on an Exodus shape: in the Last Days the Jews will depart from the lands of their exile and return to an earthly Zion. Hence Exodus politics and political messianism are radically entangled in Zionist thought. The tangle is nicely symbolized in a dream that Theodor Herzl, late in his life, recounted to a friend: he was twelve years old and dreamt that the "King-Messiah" appeared and

> took me in his arms and carried me off on wings of heaven. On one of the iridescent clouds we met . . . Moses. (His features resembled those of Michelangelo's statue. As a child I loved . . . this marble portrait.) The Messiah called

out to Moses, "For this child I have prayed!" To me, he said, "Go and announce to the Jews that I shall soon come and perform great and wondrous deeds for my people and for all mankind."[4]

It is the prophet Moses, not David the king, who hovers in the background of this messianic vision and suggests the nature of the deeds to come. If Herzl, a worldly man and a Jew thoroughly assimilated to secular culture, remembered dreams of this sort, we can assume that they played an even larger part among the Orthodox masses of Eastern Europe. Clearly Zionism drew upon messianic faith and messianic energy—even when the political activity it required was prosaic, repetitious, endlessly frustrating. But the Exodus parallel was closer. The opposition that Herzl encountered and the manifest refusal of most Jews to leave their homes in exile and set out for the promised land looked much more like the familiar troubles of Moses than the foretold triumphs of the messiah. It was not an accident that in Herzl's dream Moses had a face, the messiah only a title and an aura.

The Exodus parallel was not lost on the most impressive of Zionist thinkers, Ahad Ha-Am ("One of the People," the *nom de plume* of Asher Ginzberg), who published an essay on Moses in 1904. This is a powerful piece, describing a leader who imagined at first that liberation would be immediate and complete but who learned in the wilderness that it would be a long and hard struggle. Ahad Ha-Am repeats Maimonides: "A people trained for generations in the house of bondage cannot cast off in an instant the effects of that training and become truly free . . . ." And he has Moses draw the conclusion that he himself drew with regard to his own contemporaries:

He no longer believes in a sudden revolution; he knows that signs and wonders and visions of God can arouse a momentary enthusiasm, but cannot create a new heart, cannot uproot and implant feelings and inclinations with any stability or permanence. So he summoned all his patience to the task of bearing the troublesome burden of his people and training it by slow steps till it is fit for its mission.[5]

We can call this Exodus Zionism and set it against the messianic Zionism that first took political form in Palestine in the 1920s. In the context of Jewish, and especially of Diaspora, history, Exodus Zionism involved what the novelist A. B. Yehoshua has called "an act of renunciation —a renunciation of messianism, religious salvation, and the vision of the End of Days."[6] This renunciation was easiest for men and women of the left, committed to a secular and socialist version of the biblical promise. A few socialists, like David Ben-Gurion, still entertained messianic hopes, but these were hopes rooted more in the prophets than in the writers of the apocalypse. Messianic Zionism was by and large the creation of the right, of the so-called Revisionists, and it is in Israel today exclusively a right-wing creed. It shares nevertheless the crucial features of a certain kind of radical politics. The first of these features is an extraordinary sensitivity to and something like a longing for apocalyptic events. Certainly, the twentieth century has been more than forthcoming: has there ever been a time that looked more like the next-to-last days than the 1930s and 1940s? The rise of nazism, the Second World War, and the destruction of European Jewry bred the desperate hope and then, among some intellectual militants in Palestine, the desperate certainty of a great transformation, a total reversal. But this would require a second and more local apocalypse. Rescued from

European destruction, these militants claimed a destruction of their own, as if in accordance with a talmudic saying about the "messianic travail": "War is the beginning of Redemption."[7] (But so is famine, familial discord, the collapse of schools and academies: none of this is meant to be programmatic.) The most extreme Revisionists, the members of the Stern Gang, "conceived of the final battle with the British as an apocalyptic catharsis out of which they could expect only death."[8] Their people, however, would win at last the political version of eternal life. "When the last British soldier left the country," one of them wrote, "messianic times would arrive."[9]

The second feature of political messianism is the readiness to "force the End"—which doesn't mean merely to act politically (rather than wait for God's mighty hand) but to act politically for ultimate purposes. Men and women who force the End take deliverance into their own hands, and it is not from any particular evil but from evil in general that they would deliver themselves and all the rest of us. They claim divine authority for their politics and effectively rule out the requirements of both morality and prudence. When the stakes are this high, it is implausible to demand any sort of restraint. Force itself is sanctified when it is used to bring about the end of days, and so it can be used without guilt. On the far right of Israeli politics in the 1970s and 1980s voices could be heard espousing an almost ecstatic messianism—the ecstasy heightened by each new Middle Eastern war, for weren't these the wars of Gog and Magog, ushering in the age of glory? God Himself seems almost to stand or fall with Israel's armies: "The victory of Israel . . . is the victory of the Divine idea, and Israel's defeat the defeat of that idea."[10]

In Exodus history military defeat is never seen in this

way; it is not God's loss but Israel's failure; it has its source in corruption and oppression, and it serves to remind the Israelites of the conditional character of the promises. But the third feature of political messianism is the claim of unconditionality. Among right-wing Zionists, according to Ernst Simon, one of their religious critics, "the covenant is being interpreted . . . as a Bill of Rights, unconnected, as it were, with the observance of religious duties."[11] The victory of 1967 posed a difficult choice for religious Jews. They could hold the newly conquered territories against all opposition, viewing the conquest as a fulfillment of God's promise to Abraham; or they could remember the Exodus command—"Thou shalt not oppress a stranger: for ye know the heart of a stranger, seeing ye were strangers in the land of Egypt" (Exod. 23:9) —and seek a political compromise. Within the terms of Exodus politics one can make an argument either way; there is much in the text that supports a harsh politics, though I am inclined to think that Simon's argument for compromise is a strong one. But within the world of political messianism the argument is foreclosed. There is no need to surrender territory for the sake of morality, for morality comes, so to speak, with the territory. Both are guaranteed. The Six Day War, writes a contemporary rabbi, was "an astounding divine miracle . . . the end of days has already come . . . behold now through conquest *Eretz Yisrael* [the land of Israel] has been redeemed from oppression. . . . it has entered the realm of sanctity."[12]

The strongest opposition to the political messianism of right-wing Zionists came from the greatest scholar of Jewish messianism, Gershom Scholem.

I absolutely deny that Zionism is a messianic movement . . . . The redemption of the Jewish people, which as a

Zionist I desire, is in no way identical with the religious redemption I hope for in the future. . . . The Zionist ideal is one thing and the messianic ideal another, and the two do not meet except in the pompous phraseology of mass rallies. . . .[13]

The decisive difference between the two for Scholem was that Zionism meant acting within history and accepting the limits of historical reality, while messianism represented a utopian refusal of those limits. "We must accept the decree of history without a utopian cover. And, obviously, one must pay for that. One encounters others who have . . . interests and rights . . . [and must] succeed in coming to terms with them."[14] Scholem called himself an Ahad Ha-Amist, which is to say that he, too, believed that the crucial struggle is the struggle in the wilderness— extended into the promised land itself—to create a free people and to live up to the terms of the covenant. "If the dream of Zionism is numbers and borders and if we can't exist without them, then Zionism will fail. . . ."[15] This is the authentic prophetic voice, remembering the Egypt of bondage and exile, hoping that Canaan, now Israel, will turn out to be a better place.

III

THERE is one moment in the Exodus story that fits or seems to fit into the radicalism of right-wing Zionists and that I have avoided until now: the conquest of the land. In Exodus politics as it has been interpreted and elaborated over the centuries, the conquest plays only a small part. It figures in the writing of some of the American

Puritans, confronting the Indians of New England, and then again among the South African Boers. But it is missing, for obvious reasons, from the political theory of liberation. If the movement from Egypt to Canaan is taken as a metaphor for a transforming politics, then attention is focused on internal rather than external wars, on the purges of the recalcitrant Israelites rather than on the destruction of the Canaanite nations. And so I have focused my own attention in this book.

Read the text as it stands, however, and there is clearly no tension between the concern for strangers and the original conquest and occupation of the land—for the Canaanites are explicitly excluded from the world of moral concern. According to the commandments of Deuteronomy they are to be driven out or killed—all of them, men, women, and children—and their idols destroyed.

> But thou shalt utterly destroy them; namely, the Hittites, and the Amorites, the Canaanites, and the Perizzites, the Hivites, and the Jebusites; as the Lord thy God hath commanded thee: that they teach you not to do after all their abominations. . . . (20:17–18)

That is straightforward enough, and it hardly matters that the conquest seems to have had in fact a very different character: more like a gradual infiltration than a systematic campaign of extermination. What matters is the law. Is it a feature of revolutionary history that newly liberated and covenanted peoples should think about their enemies in this absolutist fashion? Political messianists, indeed, treat all opposition as the work of Satan, but Satan makes no appearance in Exodus history; the abominations of the Canaanites are their own work, human, all-too-human. The struggle for Canaan is not like the wars of Gog and Magog; perhaps that's why it could, in the event, lead to a rough accommodation. But God was dissatisfied with the accommodation (see Judg. 2:1–3); He wanted an all-out war against idolatry and idolators. I think it is fair to describe this war as an extension of the struggles in the wilderness. Revolutionary wars take on something of the ferocity of civil wars and political purges, even when the enemy is not satanic and the end of days is not at hand. But the people are reluctant warriors; they, or many of them, prefer peace. So the divine commandment and the failure of the Israelites to fulfill the commandment are, both of them, further examples of biblical realism.

There are signs in the text of some anxiety about the conquest commands—a search for reasons, lest God's wrath seem wholly arbitrary.[16] But reasons are dangerous. If the Canaanites were condemned because they were idolators, because of their "abominations," as Leviticus and Deuteronomy suggest, won't the Israelites, backsliding into idolatry, be treated in the same way? The biblical writers were (and knew they were) establishing a precedent that might one day be used against their own people: "As the nations which the Lord destroyeth before your face, so shall ye perish; because ye would not be obedient unto the voice of the Lord your God" (Deut. 8:20). Because of this parallelism, perhaps, the commandment, "Thou shalt utterly destroy them," does not survive the work of interpretation; it was effectively rescinded by talmudic and medieval commentators arguing over its future applications. If there was another Exodus, would there be another conquest—and would the inhabitants of the promised land once again be placed under the ban? The commandment applied, the commentators argued, only to specific groups of people, named in the text, who no longer exist or can no longer be recognized. "Sennacherib the King of Assyria came," wrote Rabbi Yehuda, invoking the biblical account of the reign of Hezekiah (2 Kings 18–19), "and confounded all the nations."[17] "Their memory," wrote Maimonides, "has long perished."[18] Hence the ban could have no practical effect; Jews returning to the land would not encounter Hittites or Amorites. Right-wing Zionists who cite the biblical passages are practicing a kind of fundamentalism that is entirely at odds with the Jewish tradition. For Judaism, like Exodus politics itself, is not found in the text so much as in the interpretations of the text.

IV

IF contemporary Zionists stand uneasily between the "door of hope" opened in the Exodus story and the fantasies of political messianism, so, more generally, do radicals and revolutionaries dream of the promised land and also of the lost garden, of Canaan and also of paradise. The analysis of radicalism as a secularized form of messianic zeal, stressing the second term in these pairs, has played a large part in modern scholarship.[19] It has, of course, a political purpose: it points to the extravagances of leftist ideology; it suggests the *hubris* of men and women who set out to do what only God can do (or so we once believed); it calls attention to the genuine madmen who live on the margins of every revolutionary movement—and who are not, perhaps, as marginal as they seem. Undoubtedly, there is truth as well as political purpose here. The translation of messianic fantasy into worldly activity is a fact of the modern age. Ideologists and militants have not only dreamt of but actually reached for a kind of secular paradise, the perfection of humankind in a perfect society: unity, harmony, freedom, eternal bliss. And they have done this in the firm expectation that paradise was the necessary and inevitable end of *our* history, a promised land, indeed, whether or not there existed a God capable of making promises. The end of history is also the abolition of history, the total destruction (not only of Canaanites but) of the familiar world and conceivably of most of the people in it—so that the surviving remnant can enter the new Jerusalem. If messianism outlives religious faith, it still inhabits the apocalyptic framework that faith established. Hence the readiness of messianic militants to welcome, even to initiate, the terrors that precede the Last Days; and hence the strange politics of *the worse, the better;* and hence the will to sin, to risk any crime for the sake of the End.

It is a serious mistake, however, a misreading of the historical record, to argue that radical politics necessarily and always takes this form. Among critics of political messianism the mistake is common and even deliberate: if they lump together every sort of radical aspiration, they do so because they see the threat of apocalyptic fanaticism all around them, lurking, as it were, in every revolutionary program. Talmon, for example, marks off two sorts of oppositionist politics. The first is traditional, "the old type of social struggle," the politics of despair, uninspired by any sort of coherent argument. His central example is the peasant *jacquerie*. "The oppressed may have nourished a vague sense of grievance and murmured not a little, but they had no program, no vision, no alternative scheme of things. These uprisings were . . . elemental outbursts."[20] I doubt that social action is ever quite so

145

"elemental," so devoid of meaning for its participants. For Talmon, however, as soon as there is a program, a vision, a scheme of things, there is also political messianism—as if Western culture provided no other model for a purposive politics. Traditional revolt and messianic revolution exhaust the field. In fact, our culture is far richer than that, and modern radicalism is predictably diverse, internally contradictory, a tangle of opposing perceptions and hopes.

Exodus history, as I have said repeatedly, is the source of messianic politics. John Canne, an English Fifth Monarchyman, writing in 1657, makes the crucial claim. "It is a common received opinion: In the Lord's bringing Israel out of Egypt was shadowed out the deliverance of his church and people from all tyranny and oppression in the last days."[21] *Shadowed out* is exactly right, and the shadows are larger than life: not Egypt but the world, not this particular tyranny but all tyranny and oppression, not the future but the Last Days. Without its shadows, however, the Exodus provides the chief alternative to messianism —as Oliver Cromwell's dispute with the Fifth Monarchy suggests. For the Exodus begins with a concrete evil and ends (or doesn't quite end) with a partial success. To be sure, the partial success is a problem. So far is the end of the story from the end of days that there is more than enough room for the backsliding and renewed oppression that repeatedly transform the hope of the Exodus into messianic fantasy. Messianism has its origins in disappointment, in all those Canaans that turn out to be "almost barren." Yet who can doubt that it is better to be in Canaan than in Egypt? And better to work for one more local deliverance than to risk the terrors of the next-to-last days? In every revolutionary movement there are men and women who want to be able to say, with Cromwell,

"We are thus far . . ."—and to know, in fact, where they are. For them, Exodus history gives rise to Exodus politics.

Compared with political messianism, Exodus makes for a cautious and moderate politics. Compared with "the old type of social struggle" or with the even more common passivity and acquiescence of the oppressed, it makes for a revolutionary politics. But these terms are misleading. As we have seen, the Exodus story is open to interpretation, and one can imagine social democrats and (some) Bolsheviks at home within it. The biblical text tells a tale of argument and contention, and the commentators read the text in the same spirit; there is always "another interpretation." Political messianism is quite different. One can calculate endlessly the number of days until the Last Days; there is always another calculation; but once a decision has been made to force the End, there is no room for argument. Then politics is absolute, enemies satanic, compromise impossible. Exodus politics slides, sometimes, toward absolutism—as in a sermon preached by the Puritan minister Stephen Marshall to the House of Commons in 1641: "All people are cursed or blessed according as they do or do not join their strength and give their best assistance to the Lord's people against their enemies."[22] The curses and blessing derive, I suppose, from Deuteronomy, but Marshall comes close to the later Bolshevik slogan, "You are either for us or against us." It's only when the struggle is an ultimate one that choice can be so radically restricted. For men and women working within the Exodus tradition, however, choice more commonly takes on a different character. There is no ultimate struggle, but a long series of decisions, backslidings, and reforms. The apocalyptic war between "the Lord's people" and "their enemies" can't readily be located within the Exodus.

Absolutism is effectively barred, I think, by the very

character of the people, frightened, stubborn, contentious, and at the same time, members of the covenant. The people can't be killed (not all of them anyway) or cast aside or miraculously transformed. They must be led, chastised, defended, argued with, educated—activities that undercut and defeat any simple designation of "enemies." The revolutionary idea of a holy nation does breed enemies, of course, but the struggle is never so melodramatic as Marshall's formula suggests. The presence of the people makes for realism, not only because some among the people are tough-minded and skeptical realists, asking hard questions, like the psalmist's "Can God furnish a table in the wilderness?" or the midrashic rabbi's "On what grounds do you slay three thousand men in one day?" The people also make for realism because the pace of the march must be set with their feelings in mind, because their rebellions must be dealt with, leaders chosen from their midst, and the law expounded in their hearing. They can't easily be divided into friends and enemies; their very stiff-neckedness is somehow admirable. Many of them still retained an affection for Egypt, wrote Benjamin Franklin in a "Comparison of the Conduct of the Ancient Jews and of the Anti-Federalists," but "on the whole it appears [from the text] that the Israelites were a people jealous of their newly acquired liberty." They were only inexperienced and, like the Americans, "worked upon by artful men. . . ."[23]

This is a typical piece of Exodus politics, but it doesn't quite suggest the sobering power of the biblical story, for Franklin was hardly disposed to think of the Anti-Federalists as the representatives of Anti-Christ. In the writings of contemporary liberation theologians, the power of the story is more evident. One can feel in their books and essays a constant thrust toward political messianism, but since Exodus is the standard reference for liberation, and the promised land the standard goal, there is also a strong sense of this-worldly complexity. Exodus history and politics work as a constraint on Christian eschatology. Liberation is not a movement from our fallen state to the messianic kingdom but from "the slavery, exploitation, and alienation of Egypt" to a land where the people can live "with human dignity." The movement takes place in historical time; it is the hard and continuous work of men and women. The best of the liberation theologians explicitly warns his readers against "absolutizing [the] revolution" and falling into idolatry toward "unavoidably ambiguous human achievements."[24] This, again, is Exodus politics.

So pharaonic oppression, deliverance, Sinai, and Canaan are still with us, powerful memories shaping our perceptions of the political world. The "door of hope" is still open; things are not what they might be—even when what they might be isn't totally different from what they are. This is a central theme in Western thought, always present though elaborated in many different ways. We still believe, or many of us do, what the Exodus first taught, or what it has commonly been taken to teach, about the meaning and possibility of politics and about its proper form:

—first, that wherever you live, it is probably Egypt;
—second, that there is a better place, a world more attractive, a promised land;
—and third, that "the way to the land is through the wilderness."[25] There is no way to get from here to there except by joining together and marching.

NOTES

INDEX

NOTES

Introduction

1. A dramatic account of an Exodus sermon plays a large part in Joseph R. Washington, *Black Religion* (Boston: Beacon Press, 1964), pp. 99–102.

2. *Oliver Cromwell's Letters and Speeches,* ed. Thomas Carlyle (London, 1893), pt. 8, pp. 19, 34.

3. Ernst Bloch, *Atheism in Christianity: The Religion of the Exodus and the Kingdom,* trans. J. T. Swann (New York: Herder and Herder, 1972).

4. Steffens, *Moses in Red: The Revolt of Israel as a Typical Revolution* (Philadelphia: Dorrance, 1926).

5. J. Severino Croatto, *Exodus: A Hermeneutics of Freedom,* trans. Salvator Attanasio (Maryknoll, N.Y.: Orbis, 1981), p. iv. For a critical account of the book of Exodus as the "privileged text" of liberation theology and an extensive bibliography of books and articles by Latin American theologians, see J. Andrew Kirk, *Liberation Theology: An Evangelical View from the Third World* (Atlanta: John Knox, 1979), esp. chaps. 8 and 14.

6. Albert J. Raboteau, *Slave Religion: The "Invisible Institution" in the Antebellum South* (New York: Oxford, 1978), p. 319.

7. Collot d'Herbois, quoted in Crane Brinton, *The Jacobins: An Essay in the New History* (New York: Macmillan, 1930), p. 101.

8. A survey of some of this literature can be found in my article "Exodus 32 and the Theory of Holy War: The History of a Citation," 61 *Harvard Theological Review* (January 1968), pp. 1–14; and see detailed references below. Lewis Feuer, *Ideology and the Ideologists* (New York: Harper Torchbooks, 1975), chap. 1, includes a resolutely hostile description of "the Mosaic revolutionary myth," with some historical examples of the influence of the myth.

Notes

9. Conrad Cherry, ed., *God's New Israel: Religious Interpretations of American Destiny* (Englewood Cliffs, N.J.: Prentice Hall, 1971), p. 65.

10. See T. Dunbar Moodie, *The Rise of Afrikanerdom: Power, Apartheid, and the Afrikaner Civil Religion* (Berkeley: University of California Press, 1975), chaps. 1 and 2.

11. Croatto, *Exodus,* p. 18.

12. On the Jewish view of interpretation, see Gershom Scholem's essay "Revelation and Tradition as Religious Categories in Judaism," in *The Messianic Idea in Judaism* (New York: Schocken, 1971), pp. 282–303.

13. Frye, *The Great Code: The Bible and Literature* (New York: Harcourt Brace Jovanovich, 1982), p. xvii; but Frye's "code" suggests too elaborate an architecture; I have learned more from the more modest readings of Robert Alter, *The Art of Biblical Narrative* (New York: Basic Books, 1981).

14. Croatto, *Exodus,* pp. 20, 23.

15. *Mekilta De-Rabbi Ishmael,* trans. Jacob Z. Lauterbach (Philadelphia: Jewish Publication Society, 1935), 1:141 (on Exod. 13:1–4).

16. James B. Pritchard, ed., *The Ancient Near East,* vol. 1, *An Anthology of Texts and Pictures* (Princeton: Princeton University Press, 1958), pp. 16–24.

17. For Rome as a promised land, see *Aeneid* 1: 234–97.

18. See the discussion of the opening chapters of the Book of Exodus in Michael Fishbane, *Text and Texture: Close Readings of Selected Biblical Texts* (New York: Schocken, 1979), chap. 4.

19. Irwin, "The Hebrews," in H. and H. A. Frankfort et al., *The Intellectual Adventure of Ancient Man* (Chicago: University of Chicago Press, 1946), pp. 318–19.

20. See the argument of Herbert N. Schneidau, *Sacred Discontent: The Bible and Western Tradition* (Baton Rouge: University of Louisiana Press, 1976), but also the qualifications urged by Alter, *Biblical Narrative,* pp. 24ff.

21. Buber, *Moses: The Revelation and the Covenant* (New York: Harper Torchbooks, 1958), p. 86. I have followed the talmudic numbering of the murmurings in treatise 'Arakin 15a, endorsed by Rashi: see *Pentateuch with Rashi's Commentary,* trans. M. Rosenbaum and A. M. Silberman (Jerusalem, 5733 [1973]), at Num. 14:24. For an alternative numbering, which would require a different interpretation, see F. V. Winnett, *The Mosaic Tradition* (Toronto: University of Toronto Press, 1949), chap. 6.

22. Morris: *Selected Writings and Designs,* ed. Asa Briggs (Harmondsworth: Penguin, 1962), p. 114.

23. See Frank E. Manuel, *Shapes of Philosophical History* (Stanford: Stanford University Press, 1965), esp. chap. 1, and Ernest Lee Tuveson, *Millennium and Utopia: A Study in the Background of the Idea of Progress* (Berkeley: University of California Press, 1949).

24. Manuel, *Shapes,* pp. 2–4, 9.

25. See, for example, Norman Cohn, *The Pursuit of the Millennium: Revolutionary Messianism in Medieval and Reformation Europe and Its Bearing on Modern Totalitarian Movements* (New York: Harper Torchbooks, 1961).

26. Saadya Gaon, *Book of Doctrines and Beliefs,* trans. Alexander Altmann, in *Three Jewish Philosophers* (Philadelphia: Jewish Publication Society, 1960), pp. 168–69.

27. W. D. Davies, *The Territorial Dimension of Judaism* (Berkeley: University of California Press, 1982), p. 61; on the return of manna, see Joseph Klausner, *The Messianic Idea in Israel: From Its Beginning to the Completion of the Mishnah,* trans. W. F. Stinespring (New York: Macmillan, 1955), pp. 343, 345.

Chapter One

1. *The Bacchae and Other Plays,* trans. Philip Vellacott (Harmondsworth: Penguin, 1954), p. 123.

2. Ibid., p. 104.

3. Joseph Vogt, *Ancient Slavery and the Ideal of Man,* trans. Thomas Wiedemann (Oxford: Basil Blackwell, 1974), p. 20.

4. *Oxford English Dictionary,* s.v. "oppress."

5. Thucydides' Melian Dialogue provides a typical example: "when, upon pressure of the enemy, their most apparent hopes fail them . . . " (5.103.2)—this is Hobbes' translation. I am grateful to my colleague, Professor Glen Bowersock, for helping me survey fifth- and fourth-century usages.

6. *OED,* s.v. "oppress."

7. See the discussion in Nehama Leibowitz, *Studies in Shemot (Exodus),* trans. Aryeh Newman (Jerusalem, 1981), 1: 39–48.

8. M. M. Austin and P. Vidal-Naquet, *Economic and Social History of Ancient Greece* (Berkeley: University of California Press, 1977), pp. 86–90.

9. Steffens, *Moses in Red: The Revolt of Israel as a Typical Revolution* (Philadelphia: Dorrance, 1926), p. 51.

10. Gustavo Gutierrez, *A Theology of Liberation: History, Politics, and Salvation,* trans. Sister Caridad Inda and John Eagleson (Maryknoll, N.Y.: Orbis, 1973), p. 156.

11. *Midrash Rabbah: Exodus,* trans. S. M. Lehrman, ed. H. Freeman and Maurice Simon (London: Soncino, 1983), 1:12 (pp. 14–15).

12. *The Code of Maimonides, Book Twelve: The Book of Acquisition,* trans. Isaac Klein (New Haven: Yale University Press, 1951), p. 247 (5.1.6); on heathen slaves, p. 281 (5.9.8). See the discussion of the latter passage

in Isador Twersky, *Introduction to the Code of Maimonides (Mishnah Torah)* (New Haven: Yale University Press, 1980), pp. 427–28.

13. Junius Brutus [Philip de Mornay?], *Vindiciae Contra Tyrannos: A Defense of Liberty Against Tyrants* (London, 1689), p. 124.

14. E. E. Urbach, "The Laws Regarding Slavery as a Source for the Social History of the Period of the Second Temple, the Mishnah and Talmud," 1 *Papers of the Institute of Jewish Studies* (1964), pp. 39–40; see also I. Mendelsohn, *Slavery in the Ancient Near East: A Comparative Study of Slavery in Babylonia, Assyria, Syria, and Palestine from the Middle of the Third Millennium to the End of the First Millennium* (London: Oxford University Press, 1949).

15. *Life of Moses* in *Philo*, trans. F. H. Colson (London: Heinemann [Loeb Classical Library], 1935), 6: 295.

16. Louis Ginzberg, *The Legends of the Jews*, vol. 2, *From Joseph to the Exodus*, trans. Henrietta Szold (Philadelphia: Jewish Publication Society, 1910), p. 247.

17. Girolamo Savonarola, *Prediche sopra l'Esodo* (Rome: A. Belaretti, 1955–56), 2 vols.; Milton, *Of Reformation, Tenure of Kings and Magistrates, Ready and Easy Way to Establish a Free Commonwealth*; sermons by George Duffield, Nicholas Street, Samuel Langdon, James Dana: see below for particular references.

18. Arendt, *On Revolution* (New York: Viking, 1963), esp. chap. 2.

19. [John Lilburne,] *England's Birth-Right Justified*, reprinted in *Tracts on Liberty in the Puritan Revolution: 1638–1647*, ed. William Haller (New York: Columbia University Press, 1933), 3:302.

20. J. Severino Croatto, *Exodus: A Hermeneutics of Freedom*, trans. Salvator Attanasio (Maryknoll, N.Y.: Orbis, 1981), p. 18 (emphasis in original).

21. Herbert N. Schneidau, *Sacred Discontent: The Bible and Western Tradition* (Baton Rouge: University of Louisiana Press, 1976), pp. 204–6; see Millard C. Lind, *Yahweh Is a Warrior: The Theology of Warfare in Ancient Israel* (Scottdale, Pa.: Herald Press, 1980), pp. 87–88 and passim, on the religious and political reasons for the rejection of chariot warfare by the Israelites.

22. The meaning has been stable for a long time now: cf. the passage in Cervantes' *Don Quixote*, where Sancho Panza is riding away from "Camacho's splendid feast and festival," leaving behind "the fleshpots of Egypt, though in his heart he took them with him"—trans. John Ormsby (Chicago: Britannica, 1952), p. 270 (2:21, last paragraph).

23. Bloch, *Atheism in Christianity: The Religion of the Exodus and the Kingdom*, trans. J. T. Swann (New York: Herder and Herder, 1972), p. 31.

24. Savonarola, *Prediche sopra l'Esodo*, 1:159 (sermon 6). I am grateful to Luisa Saffioti, who provided me with a translation of the Savonarola sermons.

25. Ginzberg, *Legends of the Jews*, 2:251; see *Midrash Rabbah: Exodus*, 1:18 (p. 25).

26. Josephus, *Of the Antiquities of the Jews* in *The Famous and Memorable Works of Josephus*, trans. Thomas Lodge (London, 1620), p. 41 (2.9.1).

27. Schneidau, *Sacred Discontent*, esp. chap. 3.

28. *Passover Haggadah*, trans. with commentary by Joseph Elias (Brooklyn: Mesorah, 1981), p. 145.

29. *Midrash Rabbah: Exodus*, 16:4 (p. 210); I have quoted the translation in Leibowitz, *Studies in Shemot*, p. 264.

30. *Midrash Rabbah: Exodus*, 1:8 (p. 10).

31. Savonarola, *Prediche sopra l'Esodo*, 1:77 (sermon 3).

32. *Midrash Rabbah: Exodus*, 1:8 (p. 10) on circumcision; *Yalkut Shimoni* (a twelfth-century Midrash), quoted in Leibowitz, *Studies in Shemot*, p. 2, on the amphitheaters.

33. *Haggadah*, ed. Elias, pp. 68, 106.

34. According to Maimonides, God recognized the sensual appeal of Egyptian idolatry to the Israelites and accommodated Himself to it: the practice of ritual sacrifice was a divine concession, "so that [the people] should be left with the kind of practices to which they were accustomed . . ." and brought only gradually to the pure worship of God. *The Guide of the Perplexed*, trans. Shlomo Pines (Chicago: University of Chicago Press, 1963), 2:525–31 (3.32.69b–73a). See the discussion in Amos Funkenstein, "Maimonides: Political Theory and Realistic Messianism," in *Miscellanea Mediaevalia*, vol. 2: *Die Mächte des Guten and Bösen* (Berlin: Walter de Gruyter, 1977), pp. 81–103; and below, on the politics of gradualism, pp. 54–55.

35. Schneidau takes Deuteronomy 7:15, "the evil diseases of Egypt, *which thou knowest . . . ,*" to mean that it was the Israelites who had suffered in Egypt (*Sacred Discontent*, p. 148n.). There is a Jewish legend to the same effect, see below, chap. 3.

36. Marshall, *A Sermon Before the Honorable House of Commons* (London, 1641), p. 31; William Perkins, *The Works* (London, 1616), 2:422.

37. *The Ready and Easy Way to Establish a Free Commonwealth* (2nd. ed., 1660), in *Complete Prose Works of John Milton*, vol. 7, ed. Robert W. Ayers (New Haven: Yale University Press, 1980), p. 463.

Chapter Two

1. Hecht, "Exile," in *Millions of Strange Shadows* (New York: Atheneum, 1977), p. 45.

2. Girolamo Savonarola, *Prediche sopra l'Esodo*, 2 vols. (Rome: A. Bela-

retti, 1955–56), 1:157–58 (sermon 6) and 1:189–90 (sermon 7); see the discussion of the second of these sermons in *The Letters of Machiavelli,* trans. Allan Gilbert (New York: Capricorn, 1961), pp. 85–89 (letter no. 3).

3. I have followed here the argument of Nehama Leibowitz, *Studies in Shemot (Exodus),* trans. Aryeh Newman (Jerusalem, 1981), 1:39–46; see *Midrash Rabbah: Exodus,* trans. S. M. Lehrman, ed. H. Freeman and Maurice Simon (London: Soncino, 1983), 1:29 (pp. 36–37) and *Pirke Aboth: The Ethics of the Talmud,* trans. R. Travers Herford (New York: Schocken, 1962), 2:6 (p. 46).

4. Elkins, *Slavery: A Problem in American Institutional and Intellectual Life* (New York: Grosset and Dunlap, 1963), chap. 3.

5. *Midrash Rabbah: Exodus,* 5:14 (p. 93); I quote the translation in Leibowitz, *Studies in Shemot,* p. 87.

6. *Pentateuch with Rashi's Commentary,* trans. M. Rosenbaum and A. M. Silberman (Jerusalem, 5733 [1973]), at Exod. 5:1.

7. See Ibn Ezra on Exod. 13:17, quoted in Leibowitz, *Studies in Shemot,* pp. 235, 244.

8. Savonarola, *Prediche sopra l'Esodo,* 2:148 (sermon 17).

9. Gad Hitchcock, quoted in Nathan O. Hatch, *The Sacred Cause of Liberty: Republican Thought and the Millennium in Revolutionary New England* (New Haven: Yale University Press, 1977), p. 63.

10. J. Severino Croatto, *Exodus: A Hermaneutics of Freedom,* trans. Salvator Attanasio (Maryknoll, N.Y.: Orbis, 1981), p. 17.

11. Joseph B. Soleveitchik, *Reflections of the Rav,* adapted by Abraham R. Besdin (Jerusalem, 1979), p. 190.

12. See the poem by Joseph Albardani (tenth-century Baghdad), "The Three Factions," in *The Penguin Book of Hebrew Verse,* ed. T. Carmi (Harmondsworth: Penguin, 1981), pp. 259–60; also Louis Ginzberg, *The Legends of the Jews,* vol. 3, *Moses in the Wilderness,* trans. Paul Radin (Philadelphia: Jewish Publication Society, 1910), p. 15.

13. Croatto, *Exodus,* p. 17.

14. Hegel, *The Spirit of Christianity,* in *On Christianity: Early Theological Writings* (New York: Harper Torchbooks, 1961), p. 190.

15. Quoted in Leibowitz, *Studies in Shemot,* p. 240.

16. Owen, *Works,* ed. W. H. Goold (New York, 1851), 8:151.

17. Nicholas Street, "The American States Acting Over the Part of the Children of Israel in the Wilderness . . . ," reprinted in Conrad Cherry, ed., *God's New Israel: Religious Interpretations of American Destiny* (Englewood Cliffs, N.J.: Prentice-Hall, 1971), p. 69.

18. John Sturdy, *The Cambridge Bible Commentary: Numbers* (Cambridge, Cambridge University Press, 1976), p. 84.

19. See the discussion in Nehama Leibowitz, *Studies in Bamidbar (Num-*

Notes

bers), trans. Aryeh Newman (Jerusalem, 1980), pp. 94–103; *Pentateuch with Rashi's Commentary*, at Num. 11:5; Ginzberg, *Legends of the Jews*, 3:246.

20. Rousseau, *The Government of Poland*, trans. Willmoore Kendall (Indianapolis: Bobbs-Merrill, 1972), p. 6.

21. *The Guide of the Perplexed*, 1:526–28 (3.32.70a and b).

22. Leibowitz, *Studies in Shemot*, p. 555.

23. Marx, *Class Struggles in France*, in *Selected Works* (Moscow, 1951), 1:193.

24. Judah Halevi, *Kuzari*, ed. Isaak Heinemann, in *Three Jewish Philosophers* (Philadelphia: Jewish Publication Society, 1960), p. 48 (1:97).

25. *Pentateuch with Rashi's Commentary*, at Exod. 32:6.

26. Ronald E. Clements, *The Cambridge Bible Commentary: Exodus* (Cambridge: Cambridge University Press, 1972), pp. 205–6. Compare U. Cassuto, *A Commentary on the Book of Exodus*, trans. Israel Abrahams (Jerusalem: The Magnes Press, 1967), pp. 408–9, who defends the integrity of the text.

27. *Life of Moses* in Philo, trans. F. H. Colson (London: Heinemann [Loeb Classical Library], 1935), 6:529; John Lightfoot, *An Handful of Gleanings out of the Book of Exodus* (London, 1643), p. 35; Steffens, *Moses in Red: The Revolt of Israel as a Typical Revolution* (Philadelphia: Dorrance, 1926), p. 103.

28. Leivy Smoler and Moshe Aberbach, "The Golden Calf Episode in Postbiblical Literature," 39 *Hebrew Union College Annual* (1968), pp. 91–116.

29. *Midrash Rabbah: Exodus*, 43:7 (pp. 502–3); I have quoted the translation in Leibowitz, *Studies in Shemot*, pp. 570–71.

30. Quoted in Albert J. Raboteau, *Slave Religion: The "Invisible Institution" in the Antebellum South* (New York: Oxford, 1978), pp. 319–20.

31. Gustavo Gutierrez, *A Theology of Liberation: History, Politics, and Salvation*, trans. Sister Caridad Inda and John Eagleson (Maryknoll, N.Y.: Orbis, 1973), pp. 156, 157.

32. See, for example, Samuel Faircloth, *The Troublers Troubled* (London, 1641), esp. pp. 22ff. and Francis Cheynell, *Sion's Momento and God's Alarum* (London, 1643), p. 19: "these are purging times. . . ."

33. Machiavelli, *The Discourses*, trans. Leslie J. Walker, revised Brian Richardson (Harmondsworth: Penguin, 1970), p. 486 (3:30). Machiavelli continues: "The need for this was clearly recognized by Friar Girolamo Savonarola."

34. Quoted from *Tanna debei Eliyahu* in Leibowitz, *Studies in Shemot*, p. 621.

35. Ramban (Nachmanides), *Commentary on the Torah: Exodus*, trans. Charles B. Chavel (New York: Shilo, 1973), pp. 567–69 (on Exod. 32:27); I have quoted the translation in Leibowitz, *Studies in Shemot*, p. 623.

36. Clements, *Commentary on Exodus*, pp. 208–9.

37. Josephus, *Of the Antiquities of the Jews* in *The Famous and Memorable Works of Josephus*, trans. Thomas Lodge (London, 1620), p. 60 (2:5:7).

38. *The Political Writings of St. Augustine,* ed. Henry Paolucci (Chicago: Henry Regnery, 1962), p. 195 (letter 93).

39. *Summa Theologica,* 2a, 2ae, Q.64, arts. 3 and 4.

40. Grotius, *The Law of War and Peace,* trans. Francis W. Kelsey (Indianapolis: Bobbs-Merrill, n.d.), p. 504 (2:22.39).

41. John Owen, *Works,* 8:156.

42. Calvin, *Sermons on the Fifth Book of Moses* (London, 1583), p. 1203.

43. Knox, *Works,* ed. D. Laing (Edinburgh, 1846–48), 3:311–12.

44. William Bridge, *A Sermon Preached Before the House of Commons* (London, 1643), p. 18.

45. *Oliver Cromwell's Letters and Speeches,* ed. Thomas Carlyle (London, 1893), pt. 8, p. 34.

46. Faircloth, *The Troublers Troubled,* pp. 24–25.

47. Steffens, *Moses in Red,* p. 108. I should note that Croatto defends revolutionary violence not by reference to Moses' purge in Exodus 32 but by reference to God's far greater violence against the Egyptians—the plagues and the overthrow at the sea: "the liberating action is necessarily violent . . . or it is prepared by none too gentle persuasive means . . ." (Croatto, *Exodus,* pp. 29–30). Similarly, Steffins refers to the last of the plagues as "God's red terror" (p. 83). But it is the purges of the Israelites, not the killing of the Egyptian firstborn, that really interest him. The plagues are more central for Croatto, who seems the most radical of the liberation theologians. See Gutierrez's rejection of violence, *Theology of Liberation,* p. 250, n. 124.

48. Buber, *Moses: The Revelation and the Covenant* (New York: Harper Torchbooks, 1958), p. 35. Cf. Lenin, *What Is to Be Done?* in *Lenin on Politics and Revolution,* ed. James E. Connor (New York: Pegasus, 1968), p. 40.

49. Ramban (Nachmanides), *Commentary on Exodus,* p. 575 (on Exod. 33:7).

50. Steffens, *Moses in Red,* p. 133.

51. *Life of Moses* in *Philo,* 6:457; Machiavelli, *The Prince,* chap. 6; Rousseau, *Government of Poland,* p. 6.

52. See Daniel Jeremy Silver, *Images of Moses* (New York: Basic Books, 1982), chap. 6.

53. Ginzberg, *Legends of the Jews,* 3:242.

Chapter Three

1. Delbert R. Hillers, *Covenant: The History of a Biblical Idea* (Baltimore: Johns Hopkins Press, 1969), chap. 2; George E. Mendenhall, *Law and Covenant in Israel and the Ancient Near East* (Pittsburgh: The Biblical Col-

loquium, 1955); John Bright, *Covenant and Promise: The Prophetic Under-standing of the Future in Pre-Exilic Israel* (Philadelphia: Westminster Press, 1976).

2. See *Passover Haggadah,* trans. with commentary by Joseph Elias (Brooklyn: Mesorah, 1981), pp. 107, 124; *Midrash Rabbah: Exodus,* trans. S. M. Lehrman, ed. H. Freeman and Maurice Simon (London: Soncino, 1983), 14:3 (p. 157); George Foot Moore, *Judaism in the First Centuries of the Christian Era: The Age of the Tannaim* (Cambridge, Mass.: Harvard University Press, 1962), 2:362–63.

3. Spinoza, *Theologico-Political Treatise* in *The Chief Works,* trans. R. H. M. Elwes (New York: Dover, 1951), 1:218–19.

4. *Midrash Rabbah: Exodus,* 28:2 (p. 332); the emphasis is the translator's.

5. Louis Ginzberg, *The Legends of the Jews,* vol. 3, *Moses in the Wilderness,* trans. Paul Radin (Philadelphia: Jewish Publication Society, 1910), p. 80ff.

6. *Mekilta De-Rabbi Ishmael,* trans. Jacob Z. Lauterbach (Philadelphia: Jewish Publication Society, 1935), 2:229–30 (on Exod. 20:2).

7. Simon Ashe, quoted in John F. Wilson, *Pulpit in Parliament: Puritanism During the English Civil Wars, 1640–1648* (Princeton: Princeton University Press, 1969), p. 174.

8. I follow here the argument of Hillers, *Covenant,* esp. chap. 5.

9. Saadya Gaon, *Book of Doctrines and Beliefs,* trans. Alexander Altmann, in *Three Jewish Philosophers* (Philadelphia: Jewish Publication Society, 1960), p. 177.

10. Wilson, *Pulpit in Parliament,* p. 199. For an account of a similar distinction in Jewish thought, see David Hartman's essay, "Sinai and Messianism," in *Joy and Responsibility: Israel, Modernity, and the Renewal of Judaism* (Jerusalem: Ben Zvi-Posner Ltd., 1978), pp. 232–58.

11. *Mekilta De-Rabbi Ishmael,* 2:207 (on Exod. 19:3–9).

12. Ginzberg, *Legends of the Jews,* 3:89.

13. The best discussion is Perry Miller, *The New England Mind: The Seventeenth Century* (Cambridge, Mass.: Harvard University Press, 1954), chap. 13.

14. See the discussion of "the freedom of the will" in Saadya Gaon, *Book of Doctrines and Beliefs,* pp. 118–21. But one famous midrashic tale qualifies the idea of freedom: "It was not quite of their own free will that Israel declared themselves ready to accept the Torah, for when the whole nation . . . approached Sinai, God lifted up the mountain and held it over the heads of the people . . . saying to them: 'If you accept the Torah, it is well; otherwise you will find your grave under this mountain.' " Ginzberg, *Legends of the Jews,* 3:92; compare *Pentateuch with Rashi's Commentary,* trans. M. Rosenbaum and A. M. Silberman (Jerusalem, 5733 [1973]) at Exod. 19:17. I take this to be, at least initially, a

piece of popular irony, but it poses a hard question: how can anyone *not* fear an omnipotent God?

15. *Book of Doctrines and Beliefs,* p. 116.

16. Quoted in Miller, *The Seventeenth Century,* p. 426.

17. The literature is immense; for a brief statement, see Walter Ullmann, *The Individual and Society in the Middle Ages* (Baltimore: Johns Hopkins Press, 1966), pp. 150–51; for a general review, see Francis Oakley, "Legitimation By Consent: The Question of the Medieval Roots," in 14 *Viator: Medieval and Renaissance Studies* (1983), pp. 303–35.

18. Sota 37b, quoted in Gordon Freeman, "The Rabbinic Understanding of Covenant as a Political Idea," in *Kinship and Consent: The Jewish Political Tradition and Its Contemporary Uses,* ed. Daniel J. Elazar (Ramat Gan, Israel: Turtledove Publishing, 1981), p. 68.

19. *The Federal and State Constitutions,* ed. F. N. Thorpe (Washington, D.C.: Government Printing Office, 1907), 3:1888–89.

20. Hillers, *Covenant,* pp. 78–79.

21. *The Passover Haggadah,* ed. Nahum Glatzer (New York: Schocken, 1969), p. 49 (emphasis in original).

22. Quoted in Nehama Leibowitz, *Studies in Devarim (Deuteronomy),* trans. Aryeh Newman (Jerusalem, 1980), p. 298.

23. Ibid., pp. 299–300.

24. *Haggadah,* ed. Elias, p. 147.

25. Hillers, *Covenant,* pp. 80–81. There is a tension in Judaism between a simple hereditary and a complex contractual view of religious obligation. This is one of the central themes of *Kinship and Consent:* see the first essay, Daniel J. Elazar, "Covenant as the Basis of the Jewish Political Tradition," pp. 41–42.

26. J. T. McNeill, *The History and Character of Calvinism* (New York: Oxford University Press, 1954), p. 142.

27. J. Severino Croatto, *Exodus: A Hermaneutics of Freedom,* trans. Salvator Attanasio (Maryknoll, N.Y.: Orbis, 1981), p. 23 (emphasis in original).

28. Gutierrez, *A Theology of Liberation: History, Politics and Salvation,* trans. Sister Caridad Inda and John Eagleson (Maryknoll, N.Y.: Orbis, 1973), p. 295.

29. Hillers, *Covenant,* pp. 125ff. See also, on the prophets and the covenant, Bright, *Covenant and Promise,* esp. chap. 3.

30. Excerpted in *Puritanism and Liberty: Being the Army Debates (1647–9) . . . with Supplementary Documents,* ed. A. S. P. Woodhouse (London: J. M. Dent, 1938), p. 208.

31. Junius Brutus [Philip de Morney?], *Vindiciae Contra Tyrannos: A Defense of Liberty Against Tyrants* (London, 1689), p. 12.

32. Ibid., pp. 26–27.

33. Goodman, *How Superior Powers Ought to Be Obeyed* (1558) (New York: Facsimile Text Society, 1931), pp. 146, 185.

34. Gutierrez, *Theology of Liberation*, p. 302.

Chapter Four

1. See Wittfogel, *Oriental Despotism: A Comparative Study of Total Power* (New Haven: Yale University Press, 1957), who has a lot to say about pharaonic Egypt but doesn't notice the biblical association between irrigation and oppression; Steffins makes the point in his *Moses in Red: The Revolt of Israel as a Typical Revolution* (Philadelphia: Dorrance, 1926), p. 131.

2. Lenin, *What Is to Be Done?* in *Lenin on Politics and Revolution*, ed. James E. Connor (New York: Pegasus, 1968), pp. 44–45.

3. *Pascal's Pensées*, intro. T. S. Eliot (New York: Dutton, 1958), no. 570, p. 157 (no translator given).

4. Abiezer Coppe, quoted in Christopher Hill, *The World Turned Upside Down: Radical Ideas During the English Revolution* (New York: Viking Press, 1972), pp. 273–74.

5. See, for example, Samuel Langdon, *The Republic of the Israelites an Example to the American State* in Conrad Cherry, ed., *God's New Israel: Religious Interpretations of American Destiny* (Englewood Cliffs, N.J.: Prentice-Hall, 1971), pp. 99, 105.

6. Gustavo Gutierrez, *A Theology of Liberation: History, Politics, and Salvation*, trans. Sister Caridad Inda and John Eagleson (Maryknoll, N.Y.: Orbis, 1975), pp. 165–67.

7. W. D. Davies, *The Territorial Dimension of Judaism* (Berkeley: University of California Press, 1982), chap. 1.

8. See the excellent discussion of the Exodus in Leo Baeck, *This People Israel: The Meaning of Jewish Existence*, trans. Albert H. Friedlander (New York: Union of American Hebrew Congregations, 1964), chap. 1.

9. Louis Ginzberg, *The Legends of the Jews*, vol. 3, *Moses in the Wilderness*, trans. Paul Radin (Philadelphia: Jewish Publication Society, 1910), p. 87.

10. See the discussion in Nehama Leibowitz, *Studies in Bamidbar (Numbers)*, trans. Aryeh Newman (Jerusalem, 1980), pp. 121–28.

11. Ginzberg, *Legends of the Jews*, 3:290–91; see the discussion of this passage in Robert J. Milch, "Korah's Rebellion," 69 *Commentary* 2 (February 1980), pp. 52–56.

12. *Midrash Rabbah: Numbers*, trans. Judah J. Slotki (London: Soncino Press, 1983), 18:6 (vol. 2, pp. 714–15).

13. *Areopagitica* (1644), in *Complete Prose Works of John Milton,* vol. 3, ed. Ernest Sirluck (New Haven: Yale University Press, 1980), pp. 555–56.

14. *Oliver Cromwell's Letters and Speeches,* ed. Thomas Carlyle (London, 1893), pt. 8, p. 355.

15. Brewer, *American Citizenship* (New York: Scribner's, 1902), p. 79.

16. Mann, *Joseph the Provider,* in *Joseph and His Brothers,* trans. H. J. Lowe-Porter (New York: Knopf, 1958), p. 980.

17. Bloch, *Atheism in Christianity: The Religion of the Exodus and the Kingdom,* trans. J. T. Swann (New York: Herder and Herder, 1972), p. 95.

18. Ibid., p. 82.

19. This is, at least in part, what Eduard Bernstein must have felt when he wrote that the movement for socialism meant everything to him and "what is usually called the final aim" nothing. *Evolutionary Socialism: A Criticism and Affirmation,* trans. Edith Harvey (New York: Schocken, 1961), p. xvii.

20. See Joseph Klausner, *The Messianic Idea in Israel: From Its Beginning to the Completion of the Mishnah,* trans. W. F. Stinespring (New York: Macmillan, 1955), pp. 19–21, 28–32.

21. Frye, *The Great Code: The Bible and Literature* (New York: Harcourt Brace Jovanovich, 1982), p. 171.

22. It is important to distinguish, as Klausner does, the messianic age from the world to come: the first has a limited duration (one can argue about its length), while the second lasts forever. I still think it correct to say that the messianic age, in its usual descriptions, will have no *history;* there will be no reason to record or distinguish events. Klausner, *Messianic Idea,* pt. 3, chap. 2.

23. Sanhedrin 98a, quoted in Gershom Scholem, "Toward an Understanding of the Messianic Idea in Judaism," in *Messianic Idea in Judaism,* (New York: Schocken, 1971), p. 13.

24. Ibid., p. 16.

25. Quoted in Klausner, *Messianic Idea,* pp. 340–41.

26. Scholem, "Toward an Understanding," pp. 1–36.

27. Berakhot 34b, quoted in Klausner, *Messianic Idea,* p. 404; Scholem, "Toward an Understanding," p. 18.

28. Quoted in Marc Saperstein, *Decoding the Rabbis: A Thirteenth Century Commentary on the Aggadah* (Cambridge, Mass.: Harvard University Press, 1980), p. 105.

29. *The Code of Maimonides, Book Fourteen: The Book of Judges,* trans. Abraham M. Hershman (New Haven: Yale University Press, 1949), pp. 240, 242 (5.12.1,4); I have quoted the translation given in Scholem, "Toward an Understanding," p. 29. See Amos Funkenstein, "Maimonides: Political Theory and Realistic Messianism," in *Miscellanea Mediaevalia,* vol. 2: *Die Mächte des Guten und Bösen* (Berlin: Walter de Gruyter,

1977), pp. 97ff., who argues that "the messianic age of Maimonides is in all its aspects a part of history, the concluding chapter in the long history of the monotheisation of the world" (p. 101)—a history that begins with the Exodus and has been throughout a gradual process.

30. Saperstein, *Decoding the Rabbis,* p. 111.

31. See Ginzberg, *Legends of the Jews,* 3:466ff. and "The Death of Moses," a series of anonymous poems dating from the eighth to the eleventh centuries, in *The Penguin Book of Hebrew Verse,* ed. T. Carmi (Harmondsworth: Penguin, 1981), pp. 266–74.

32. Daniel Jeremy Silver, *Images of Moses* (New York: Basic Books, 1982), p. 20, and chap. 1 generally.

33. *Pentateuch with Rashi's Commentary,* trans. M. Rosenbaum and A. M. Silberman (Jerusalem, 5733 [1973]), at Exod. 18:21.

34. The tension is most clearly seen in the rebellion of Dathan and Abiram, leaders of the tribe of Reuben (Jacob's firstborn): Num. 16: 1–33.

35. See, for example, John Eliot, *The Christian Commonwealth; or, The Civil Policy of the Rising Kingdom of Jesus Christ* (London, 1659), which is devoted to an exposition of Exod. 18.

36. Spinoza, *Theologico-Political Treatise,* in *The Chief Works,* trans. R. H. M. Elwes (New York: Dover, 1951), chap. 17.

37. Paine, *Common Sense,* ed. Isaac Kramnick (Harmondsworth: Penguin, 1982), p. 76.

38. Quoted in Nathan O. Hatch, *The Sacred Cause of Liberty: Republican Thought and the Millennium in Revolutionary New England* (New Haven: Yale University Press, 1977), p. 159.

39. *Republic of the Israelites,* p. 93ff. See an earlier sermon of Langdon's, to the Provincial Congress of Massachusetts in 1775: "Let them who cry up the divine right of kings consider that the only form of government which had a proper claim to a divine establishment was so far from including the idea of a king, that it was a high crime for Israel to ask to be in this respect like other nations. . . ." Quoted in Joseph Gaer and Ben Siegel, *The Puritan Heritage: America's Roots in the Bible* (New York: Mentor, 1964), pp. 50–51.

40. This is one of the main points of Scholem's essay, "Toward an Understanding."

Conclusion

1. Frank and Fritzie Manuel, *Utopian Thought in the Western World* (Cambridge, Mass.: Harvard University Press, 1979), p. 687.

Notes

2. J. L. Talmon, *The Origins of Totalitarian Democracy* (New York: Praeger, 1960), pp. 1–13.

3. MacDonald, *The Socialist Movement* (New York: Holt, 1911), p. 246.

4. Quoted in Amos Elon, *Herzl* (New York: Holt, Rinehart and Winston, 1975), p. 16.

5. *Selected Essays of Ahad Ha-Am*, trans. Leon Simon (New York: Atheneum, 1970), pp. 320, 323.

6. "Let Us Not Betray Zionism," in *Unease in Zion*, ed. Ehud Ben Ezer (New York: Quadrangle, 1974), p. 329.

7. Megillah 17b, quoted in Uriel Tal, "The Land and the State of Israel in Israeli Religious Life," 38 *Proceedings of the Rabbinical Assembly* (1976), p. 9.

8. David Biale, *Gershom Scholem: Kabbalah and Counter-History*, 2nd ed. (Cambridge, Mass.: Harvard University Press, 1982), p. 101.

9. Geula Cohen, *Woman of Violence*, trans. Hillel Halkin (New York: Holt, Rinehart and Winston, 1966), pp. 269–70.

10. Rabbi Yehudah Amital, quoted in Tal, "The Land and the State," pp. 10–11.

11. "The Arab Question as a Jewish Question," in *Unease in Zion*, p. 313. See also David Hartman, "Sinai and Messianism," in *Joy and Responsibility: Israel, Modernity, and the Renewal of Judaism* (Jerusalem: Ben Zvi-Posner Ltd., 1978) pp. 232–58.

12. Rabbi O. Hadya, quoted in Tal, "The Land and the State," p. 10.

13. Quoted in Biale, *Scholem*, p. 100.

14. Scholem, "Zionism—Dialectic of Continuity and Rebellion," in *Unease in Zion*, pp. 269–70.

15. Biale, *Scholem*, p. 104.

16. See W. D. Davies, *The Territorial Dimension of Judaism* (Berkeley: University of California Press, 1982), pp. 15–16, and Dan Jacobson, *The Story of the Stories: The Chosen People and Its God* (New York: Harper and Row, 1982), pp. 31ff.

17. Yadayim 4.4 and Berakhot 28a, quoted in Simon, "Arab Question," p. 314.

18. *The Code of Maimonides*, Book Fourteen: *The Book of Judges*, trans. Abraham M. Hershman (New Haven: Yale University Press, 1949), p. 217 (5.5.4).

19. See, for example, Talmon, *Totalitarian Democracy* and *Political Messianism: The Romantic Phase* (New York: Praeger, 1960); Norman Cohn, *The Pursuit of the Millennium: Revolutionary Messianism in Medieval and Reformation Europe and Its Bearing on Modern Totalitarian Movements* (New York: Harper Torchbooks, 1961); Guenter Lewy, *Religion and Revolution* (New York: Oxford University Press, 1974); and Lewis Feuer, *Ideology and the Ideologists* (New York: Harper Torchbooks, 1975).

Notes

20. *Political Messianism,* p. 26.

21. John Canne, *The Time of the End* (London, 1657), p. 212.

22. Marshall, *Meroz Cursed* (London, 1641), p. 9.

23. *The Works of Benjamin Franklin,* ed. John Bigelow (New York: Putnam's, 1904), 11:383, 386.

24. Gustavo Gutierrez, *A Theology of Liberation: History, Politics, and Salvation,* trans. Sister Caridad Inda and John Eagleson (Maryknoll, N.Y.: Orbis, 1973), pp. 294, 238; see also the critique of "politico-religious messianism," p. 236.

25. Davies, *Territorial Dimension,* p. 60.

INDEX

Index

Index